The Real Food Cookbook

The Real Food Cookbook

Ethel H.
Renwick

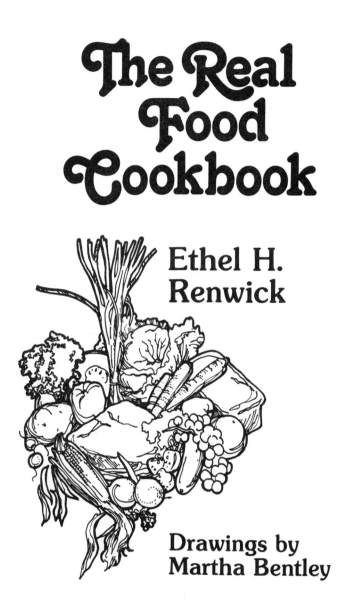

Drawings by
Martha Bentley

ZONDERVAN
PUBLISHING HOUSE OF THE ZONDERVAN CORPORATION
GRAND RAPIDS, MICHIGAN 49506

Unless otherwise indicated, Scripture references in New Testament are from *The New International Version* New Testament, © 1973 by New York Bible Society. Old Testament references are from *Revised Standard Version*.

THE REAL FOOD COOKBOOK
© 1978 by The Zondervan Corporation
Grand Rapids, Michigan

Third printing 1980

Library of Congress Cataloging in Publication Data

Renwick, Ethel Hulbert.
    The real food cookbook.

    Bibliography: p.
    Includes index.
    1. Cookery (Natural foods)   2. Nutrition.
3. Stewardship, Christian.   I. Title.
TX741.R46   641.5′63   77-27821
ISBN 0-310-31871-8

Printed in the United States of America

Contents

Preface

This cookbook has been a joy to compile not only because it consists of family recipes, but because it has been written out of deep concern for the multitude of Christians who don't realize they are missing the tremendous benefits and exquisite flavors available in the natural foods God created for our mental and physical well-being.

This book was not written for cooks who merely dabble in all kinds of cooking with no serious thought to improving the quality of their food. Rather, it has been written to alert the reader to our Christian responsibility in the care of the bodies God gave us; to explain what is wrong with many of the foods we eat today; and to point the way to a new adventure in healthful cooking.

The opening chapter, therefore, deals with our nutritional dilemma today, so that we may understand it and steer clear of its damaging traps. Succeeding chapters tell explicitly which foods to include in our daily diet and which to avoid. From there on the cook will find many recipes for breakfast and brunch; for lunch, lunch pails, and brown bags; for dinner; for beverages; and for snacks.

Because most of us are called on to cook in quantity from time to time, I have included some recipes for this purpose. They are listed as such in the index. I hope these recipes will be an encouragement to those who always cook in large quantities to pursue the subject of quantity cooking with natural foods.

The recipes in this book come from my family's kitchens — those of my two sons, my daughter, and my own — and they represent years of pleasure in experimentation with natural foods. Many of the recipes are original, but some are either basic or well-known recipes that have been converted to the extent of substituting natural and pure ingredients for the refined and the synthetic.

Most of us do not eat as many organ meats and fish as we should for maximum nutrition, so I have purposely included a variety of recipes using these foods.

My hope is that the approach and organization of this cookbook will encourage you to revise your old family favorites and to experiment creatively with new dishes.

When we speak of natural foods, we are speaking of quality. We want to furnish the cells of the bodies God gave us with the highest quality foods—the unadulterated foods He provided for our growth, health, resistance, energy, and usefulness, bearing in mind the Scripture: "So whether you eat or drink or whatever you do, do it all for the glory of God" (1 Cor. 10:31).

Water Chestnuts

Leeks

Peas

What Is Real Food?

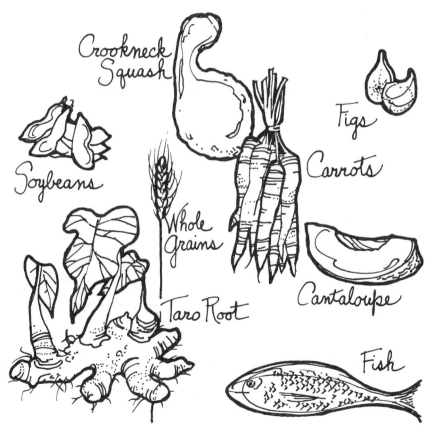

Crookneck Squash

Figs

Soybeans

Carrots

Whole Grains

Cantaloupe

Taro Root

Fish

What we eat and how we prepare what we eat directly affects both our mental and physical health. There are tomes of evidence corroborating this fact. Yet, we as a nation eat a great deal of food which does not properly nourish the cells of our bodies. We shouldn't wonder, therefore, that our degenerative diseases and mental health problems are mounting at an alarming rate.

The question is, What exactly are we eating today and why isn't it producing the most beneficial results in our bodies? Probably the most significant answer is that great changes have been made in our food, and our bodies are not handling these changes very well.

From the creation of man, human bodies assimilated natural foods. These were obviously the foods the Creator provided for human growth and health. Just as obvious was the fact that man's intricate internal mechanisms were designed to handle these natural foods efficiently so that the human body could utilize all the available vitamins, minerals, enzymes, coenzymes, and other food factors, including fiber, in a way that enabled human bodies to function properly. When farming came into existence, about ten or fifteen thousand years ago, it was done in harmony with nature. The farmer observed and respected nature's cycle of fertilization and growth, and as a result man still ate natural foods.

Today it is a different story. We have made sudden and radical changes in our food production, preparation, and consumption. These changes have all come within the last few generations and have accelerated greatly in just the past generation. When we consider all of human history, a few generations is an extremely short period of time. Only within the last few generations have our systems had to cope with changed foods and with what passes as food. In the perspective of the entire span of human life on earth, these changes are tantamount to a shock to our bodies.

Somehow in the rush of technology, we have lost sight of God's natural order for the health of all life—plant, animal, and human. God's creation has integrity. We must recapture this truth and act on it if we are to survive.

We were born to cooperate in every way with God and His

creation. Nature provides life for the rest of nature; all of life is life-giving. God's plan is an exquisite formula: a cycle of giving and receiving. This is true in the natural and physical realms as well as in the spiritual realm. God is generous, and His purpose in all things is growth—physical and spiritual. Therefore, the quality of giving and receiving must be genuine to produce growth; it must be intrinsically good; it must be real.

When man works outside of the normal cycle designed by the Creator, he destroys the very environment, outer and inner, that sustains him and that leads to the normal growth of each link of the cycle. Physical, mental, and spiritual abnormalities occur. The false, the synthetic, the less-than-real cannot produce the abundant life God wants for His creation: the bountiful life of vegetation, of animals, of humans, and of the spirit. All of creation works intricately and inextricably together; it is integrated, sane, balanced.

The history of mankind is studded with bleak periods when man tried to become master of his soul and of nature. He turned away from God or to false gods, and he cut down the forests, overgrazed the land, killed the wildlife, and let the ensuing erosion rob the farmlands of fertility. We are told that this is the way many of our deserts were formed. Today we do the same thing, but much quicker and more extensively through burgeoning technology.

Technology is the new god of the Western world. Whatever Technology dictates we are expected to follow. The new god is born of the old god, Money, the patriarch, the decision-maker. And when profit is the criterion, too often constructive developments are not sorted out from potentially destructive ones.

Today we are trying to outwit God's design for harmony, health, and growth because money doesn't come in fast enough to suit man's lust. Man wants the quick solution, although it may ultimately lead to his own deterioration and destruction.

I heard a pastor define *lust* as, "I want it, and I want it right now." In other words, a desire can be normal, healthy, and altogether a part of God's plan, but the means by which the desire is satisfied may not be in cooperation with God's wise timing. Today's technology has supplied us with many quick but temporary answers to our appetites. Lust asks, "How much money will it bring?" not, "Is it intrinsically good? Is it real? Is it according to God's exquisite order?" Industry wants to satisfy the immediate appetites, the lusts. It wants the biggest, the fanciest, the most, so that people will buy.

Specifically, what has technology done to our food, or what industry likes to call "food"?

Starting at the farming level, we have depleted our soil and turned to chemical farming—chemical fertilizers, chemical pesticides, chemical insecticides—all varying in content from one manufacturer to another. Natural fertilizer is also ultimately reduced to chemicals, but to the right chemicals and to the right complement of chemicals. Natural fertilizers are not limited to the chemicals man has decided to include, nor simply to the elements man happens to have discovered. Industry's formulas are partial, often inadequate, often synthetic, and often wrong. They are designed for specific and limited conditions. Furthermore, the chemicalized soil becomes more and more depleted and requires more and more chemicals; the end result: a dust bowl. It is not the answer to feeding the nation and the world on either an adequate or a sustained basis.

Man, through technology, endeavors to support the over-populated sections of the world. The time comes, however, when the soil is depleted; then comes the collapse of society. It has happened throughout history, but the government would have us believe that industrial technology goes on forever. This is a total oversight of history and lack of cooperation with creation.

Now our government wants to export our agricultural techniques to underdeveloped countries and lead them down the same road of vulnerability. Nations who adopt our techniques will not only be creating a need for more energy and further depleting the supplies of fossil fuel, but they will also have to depend increasingly on the false god Money. American farmers are heavy users of energy. Great quantities of energy are needed to manufacture commercial fertilizers alone. It takes money to buy oil, chemicals, and equipment.

On top of the complications of cost and energy, the strains

of grain developed for those countries are created to combat their indigenous problems. This means they are so tailored to the chemicals which fertilize them and the weather conditions the technologists expect, that if money is not available, if oil is cut off, or if weather conditions change, farming comes to an abrupt halt. They do not grow strains that are sturdy and resistant to a variety of conditions. Furthermore, when the tailored crop is harvested, it does not contain the protein and other nutritive values of normal crops.

Consequently, in teaching the underdeveloped nations how to circumvent the natural cycle, instead of how to cooperate with it, we have not helped at all. For the benefit of all mankind, we must learn that the natural cycle has no end and, if allowed to operate, increases fertility and abundance.

Besides the depletion of the soil caused by highly technical industrialization, the nutritive value of the crops themselves is depleted. The produce may be huge, but its nutrient content is not the same as produce grown by natural methods. The tomato, developed by agri-business, for example, has less nutritive value and is thick-skinned, hard, and flavorless. The naturally grown and harvested tomato is not only free from insecticides and pesticides, and incidentally also free from unfriendly bugs, but is beautiful in color and texture; it is succulent; and it is packed with optimal nutritive value.

Technology, in its push for quantity, runs into other problems besides less nutrition, such as in the natural storage of produce. For example, the developed strain of corn has a big, heavy yield. At the end of the season, however, it does not dry naturally on the stalk so that it can be stored. The vicious unnatural cycle is called on to take over; farmers have to dry the corn using more fossil fuel energy, which depletes our resources and takes money.

We see, then, that feeding the nation and the world with food worth eating, real food, requires farming on the right basis of balance: God's exquisite formula. Today it is called "organic gardening."

Technology has also moved quickly in changing the natural order in raising animals. It has shunned God's natural order of wholesome pastures, plenty of room to roam, and humane treatment. Natural methods are too slow to be as lucrative as man desires. The "I want it and I want it now" principle has taken over.

Animals bring more money when they are heavy—the earlier and the greater the weight, the more money. What better excuse for technology to find a way to circumvent the natural order for life, health, and growth? The solution is to feed animals sophisticated mixtures of overly concentrated feed and to confine them inhumanely in crowded quarters. This departure from the healthfulness of proper pasturing causes the type of stress that leads to a breakdown of natural defense systems, which is not seen under normal conditions.

The poor resistance of these animals, therefore, makes another chain in the unnatural cycle for animals; consequently, antibiotics and other drugs are given as a routine part of their diet. Even calves are given antibiotics in their milk. We are not supposed to blink an eye. We are to assume that technology knows best! We are supposed to convince ourselves that we are very fortunate, even though we may not know fully for another generation or more what defying the natural order does to our bodies and to other aspects of creation.

Thus, the natural cycle has been unconscionably broken again and again, while able and conscientious biochemists, nutritionists, and organic farmers have been trying to warn us about the undesirable, even dangerous, consequences of such practices. And all the while medical science is trying to solve the rising incidence of degenerative diseases and alarming increase in mental problems.

It is unfortunate that the initiators of the newly adopted farming methods run down the organic movement and, at the same time, run down the people who are taking steps toward God's way of life for us. They also try to denigrate those who believe in natural foods. The reason for this is that the change in food only starts with the growing of it; technology has turned its ingenuity to processing foods after they leave the field, and industry would like to dictate to us what we eat.

Industry demanded that food, or something which could pass for food, be produced as cheaply as possible and not spoil in the normal length of time; spoilage was profit-robbing and must be delayed. Industry also stipulated that products be colorful and taste sweet to entice the public. Technology met the demand in hundreds of ways. Hence the refining and the extremes of food processing.

Since the high-speed roller mill came into existence over a hundred years ago, grain has been stripped of its life, the germ, which is packed with body-building elements; and it has been stripped of its fiber, which is so necessary to proper functioning of our systems. Sugar is extracted from its context of nutrients and fiber which make up plant life and is concentrated in a form not intended in the natural cycle for human consumption. More recently, all sorts of nutrient-robbing processes have come into being: hydrogenating, hydrolyzing, texturizing, modifying, and many others.

Processing brought the advent of thousands of additives. Industry is especially enthusiastic about additives—they facilitate manufacturing, mask deterioration, make low-grade ingredients more palatable, and lengthen shelf life—all money-making procedures. Included in the additives which bring especially high profits are artificial colors and flavors which appear in an overwhelming number of canned and packaged goods today. Synthetic chemicals are substituted for the real colors and flavors because they are much cheaper.

There are literally thousands of additives. Some additives are food themselves and are harmless. Most, however, are not food; they are synthetic, and many are in question. Not all additives are tested, and none are tested in relationship to each other, yet they appear in long lists on a great many products. The very agencies which are set up to protect us and guarantee the safety of foods have failed us in some ways. One example is Red Dye #2, which was allowed to permeate literally hundreds of foods for many years. It has finally been banned because it is potentially harmful, yet it had been approved all that time. Concerning other complex chemicals, there is no way of knowing the numerous possible reactions they may have on the human body.

Some additives alter the biological structure of food itself, and some interfere with our vital processes. For example, it has been found that additives are the cause of a considerable amount of hyperactivity in children. What they are doing to adults will no doubt be an unfolding revelation as well.

Synthetic vitamins and a less easily assimilated form of iron are among the additives used in processed foods, and industry has welcomed them heartily. They are cheap and sound so nutritious—what a great sales pitch!

The fact that many vitamins and the majority of minerals, trace minerals, enzymes, coenzymes, and other factors now found to be essential to both mental and physical health are not present in highly processed foods doesn't seem to bother industry at all. But it does bother the cells of our bodies. These processed foods are not whole foods; they are not real food.

Then we come to foodless foods. These fabricated foods contain perhaps a smidgen of gelatin or dry milk solids while the rest of the ingredients are chemicals pretending to be food. Sometimes they contain fractured foods—foods which have been so altered as not to resemble food. They are foods from which molecules have been extracted and chemically treated so they may be readily manipulated to suit the manufacturer's scheme for their use. These molecules in turn become a set of molecules divorced from their context. They are not real foods. Real food is 100 percent food, and its finest source is a part of the natural, organic cycle.

It is essential for those of us who serve food to appreciate the importance of the quality of food we purchase and why we should encourage organic farming. In order to pass on information that may be useful to my readers, I asked an organic gardener why he believed in organic gardening.

He began by telling me that organic gardening is fun and also educational. He said that you learn about nature, which is enlightening, and about all sorts of life processes, including

your own body. "You learn about God and about His creation as it is in the New Testament. You learn about how we are to relate to God, to nature, to our fellow-man, and to ourselves and about the proper care and treatment of one another. The individual has his own life, but his behavior can benefit the whole species."

He went on to explain that in organic gardening you learn about God's bounty and about constructive cooperation. The principle of nature is that if you help your fellow-man, you help yourself; and in doing what's right for yourself, you help your fellow-man. He said, "That concern is built into the natural process—God set it up that way: concern for the effect each has on another for the good of itself, its fellow-beings, its environment, and the future health of all. It's all a built-in concern. It is God's plan, His dynamic."

This organic gardener went on to say that within nature at all levels the weak succumb to the strong. This means that the healthier plants are, the less likely they are to succumb to disease. The goal, then, is healthy plants, not plants that have to be protected with insecticides and pesticides. Thus, your produce comes from natural processes of fertilizing and compatible planting rather than from the instant method of chemical farming. He believes that the theory of the survival of the fittest, in the sense of being vicious, combative, and competitive, "is an aggressive human notion—God and nature are not that way at all. The natural process means cooperation toward health and strength. Nature wants to produce; it is abundant."

Basically the practice of natural agriculture (organic gardening) calls for all wastes to be recycled through soil. The gardener explained: "Soil has the ability to process huge amounts of *natural* wastes. But what does man do? He takes his wastes and puts them into water—rivers, lakes, and oceans. Water is not a medium for wastes so it can't handle them. It becomes toxic instead of beneficial. Here again, man is leaving out and going around the natural processes to get a single, short-sighted result. Inevitably, all is toxic, destructive to living cells and organisms, and not beneficial."

The earth is generous, maintained this organic gardener. "For example," he said, "six ounces of peas harvest twelve pounds. The increase is thirty-two times in seventy days. It is 'the seed that falls into fertile ground.' Just as fertile ground spiritually produces abundantly, so it is in nature. Nature is one with God; it is a reflection of God and is abundant. One-quarter ounce of spinach seeds harvests twenty-three pounds of spinach, an increase of one hundred. It reminds us of the parable of the sower whose produce was a hundredfold. God created this earth, setting up a system that was abundant and self-perpetuating; and man just runs it down to satisfy his own immediate desires. It must grieve Him."

This organic gardener concluded by saying that every year the soil gets more and more fertile when natural processes are respected. Each year the plants get healthier and produce more, and, because they are intrinsically healthy, they impart health. You are the recipient of all the nutrition God intended for you through plants."

I know this is true. I have eaten year after year from his garden—this organic gardener is my son. "The solution," he says, "is to get back to the earth; this is being responsive to the natural aspect of God."

Mango

Foods to Avoid

The first step to take to improve your diet and your health is to read the labels on every package, can, and frozen food product before you buy. Then eliminate the following:

Refined flour. This is used in many products: cereals, flours, bakery goods, pastas, mixes, convenience foods, and snack foods.

Sugar. This includes brown sugar and raw sugar; they are concentrated sugars and are not natural. Unfortunately, an unbelievable assortment of packaged and canned foods contain sugar. Sometimes sugar will be at the top of the list, showing its predominance in the product.

Additives. Only products that contain harmless food additives or chemicals you know are safe should be purchased.

Hydrogenated oils, as well as foods which contain them.

Convenience foods.

Artificial foods.

Imitation dairy products.

Refined honey.

Process cheese.

Products that list such processes as "textured," "hydrogenated," "hydrolyzed," "modified," etc.

Vegetables and fruits that have been treated with insecticides, pesticides, dyes, waxes, etc.

Animals that have been fed drugs and hormones.

Bacon, sausage, and other (cured) meats with nitrates, nitrites, and other additives. Additive-free products are available in some parts of the country.

Before you accept such statements as, "All additives are safe," "The latest agricultural technology is the only solution for today's gardeners," "The American diet is the best in the world," "To maintain good health, just be sure to eat something from the four major categories of food," "You can get your vitamins for the day from certain cereals," etc., make your own investigation. Look into the source of your information. Advertising misleads and misrepresents; many nutritionists work for the industries and write for their benefit; some nutrition foundations are funded by the sugar and cereal industries; and most medical doctors have not studied nutrition.

We Christians have been misled too long through decep-

Potatoes

Jerusalem Artichoke

tive advertising, misrepresentation, misinformation, and withheld information. We need not be misled any longer because reams of information are available on the relationship between what we eat and our mental and physical health.*

Lastly, beware of foods which are advertised as "nutritious." Read the labels to see if they really are. Industry is capitalizing on the word. For example, many "natural" breads and cereals contain sugar (usually brown sugar) and sometimes additives as well.

Very simply, we know that that which is natural, whole, and pure is real and is a part of God's creation.

*A recommended reading list appears at the end of the book.

Quince

Bread

Sprouting Seeds

Foods to Include

Beets

Cheese

Milk

Eggs

Meat

Dulse

Oranges

Corn

Bulgur

Honey

Pumpkin Seeds

Cabbage

You are in for a happy surprise when you embark on the use of natural foods and proper cooking. Good nutrition and better health are not the only dividends to be realized; there are many taste treats in store. For example, the large variety of whole grains in themselves lend enticing interest to your cereals, breads, cakes, pastas, and sauces. Nuts, seeds, and sprouting seeds add texture and character to salads, sandwiches, and vegetable dishes. Properly prepared vegetables and fruits are far more flavorful and colorful. As taste buds become educated to real foods, you will find that what you once considered normal food is actually not normal; it is sweeter and usually saltier or more highly seasoned than it should be.

The following foods should be included in wholesome diets:

Poultry and meat, if possible from organic farms.

Fish from safe waters.

Vegetables and fruits likewise are best when organically grown. Sometimes natural food stores carry produce, and sources are often advertised in the magazines sold in these stores. Another source of information is *The Organic Directory,* which is published by Rodale Press in Emmaus, Pennsylvania.

Whole-grain products cover many foods which are a part of our daily diet, such as, cereals, bakery goods, pastas, and snacks. These products should be made of whole grains or of 100-percent, stone-ground, whole-grain flours.

Whole-grain flours come in small packages; this makes it convenient to have an assortment on hand. Keep them in your refrigerator drawer or lined up in a pan in your refrigerator. There are numerous stone-ground, whole-grain flours available, such as, whole wheat, wheat germ, rye, brown rice, soybean, oat, barley, buckwheat, and triticale (a combination of wheat and rye). Potato flour should be included in an assortment of flours, as well as such meals as stone-ground corn meal.

Natural sweeteners are not only nutritious but delicious. Among them are raw, unfiltered honey, unsulphured molasses, pure fruit syrups, pure maple syrup, and date sugar (ground dates). Of the honeys, clover honey is the mildest in flavor, which may be important for certain recipes.

Dairy products that are the most nutritious are certified or licensed raw milk (not available in some states), pure creamery butter, fertile eggs (available from some farms and in some natural food stores), natural cheeses, pure yogurt, and kefir (a yogurt-type drink).

Oils should be properly processed vegetable oils. They are nutritionally important and, for this reason, care should be taken in selecting them.

Oils must be of good quality and processed as little as possible; processing robs oils of their highest nutritive value. Also, there should be no preservatives added to the oils. Commercial oils are extracted by the use of petroleum-based solvents, which some experts believe may leave carcinogenic residues. These oils are not only subjected to high heat in the refining process, which robs them of important nutritional factors, but are further altered through the addition of preservatives.

Purchase pressed, crude, or unrefined oils. *Pressed* means that the oil is extracted by pressure rather than by chemicals. *Crude* and *unrefined* mean the oils are filtered, rather than treated with chemicals, for refinement. The term *coldpressed* is not altogether accurate. Except for olives and sesame seeds, all vegetables require some heat before they will yield their oils. It is the high heat, the chemicals, and the preservatives used in commercial oils that are to be avoided.

For the above reasons, avoid commercial salad dressings and mayonnaise. These are best made at home; but dressings made with pressed oils and with no additives are available at natural food stores.

Safflower, sunflower, and sesame oils are mild in flavor; olive oil has a distinctive flavor but is excellent in salad dressings and other dishes, while peanut oil is a favorite for the stir-fry cooking of the Orient. Unrefined corn germ oil and soy oil are strong in flavor. There are numerous other oils to try, as well as some of the blended oils. Except for olive oil, which oxidizes less rapidly than other oils, all oils should be refrigerated after opening.

Thickening agents that are nutritious are whole-grain flours such as whole wheat, rye, oat, and brown rice, cornstarch, arrowroot, potato flour or potato starch, egg yolks, and pure gelatin or agar-agar. Arrowroot may be purchased by the pound at a considerable savings.

Leavening agents are found naturally in eggs and yeast or a sourdough starter. One egg is equal to ½ teaspoon of baking powder. If baking powder is used, purchase only the low-sodium type, which is free of both sodium and aluminum.

Beverages are available which are free of caffeine, theo-bromine, tannic acid, and other undesirable elements. There is a large and attractive variety of herb teas, and there are also beverages made of grains, which can substitute for coffee. Carob powder can substitute for cocoa. All these beverages are nutritious.

For those who wish to grind their own grains, nuts, and seeds, grinders which make small quantities quickly are available at many natural food stores. Also available for home use are small flour mills.

Rules for Exchange

Flour:	⅞ cup whole wheat pastry flour = 1 cup white flour
	¾ cup whole-wheat flour = 1 cup white flour
Honey:	Use half as much honey as sugar. In baking, use 2 tablespoons less liquid for each ½ cup honey.
Maple syrup:	1¼ cup maple syrup = 1 cup sugar
Chocolate:	3 tablespoons carob powder plus 2 tablespoons water or milk = 1 ounce chocolate
Butter:	The cholesterol content of butter may be reduced by whipping ½ cup safflower oil into 1 pound softened butter.

Some recipes call for wine. Wine has been used traditionally in cooking throughout much of the world because it adds flavor and, like yogurt, lemon juice, and vinegar in marinades, it acts as a tenderizer. The alcohol content of wine evaporates in cooking, even below the boiling point, so only the flavor and aroma remain. The wine in a recipe may be omitted, however, if desired. Lemon juice, vinegar, and either purple or white grape juice may be used where beneficial. Yogurt is extremely satisfactory in marinades.

Brewer's Yeast

Soybeans

Wheat Germ

How to Add Nutrition to Meals

Apple Cider Vinegar

Yogurt

Nonfat Dry Milk

Mung Beans & Sprouts

The greatest help in starting to eat more healthful foods is to keep on hand those foods which may be easily incorporated into your daily diet and which will add greater nutrition to every meal. I will suggest a few and give brief descriptions of the food as explained by some of our most experienced nutritionists.

Brewer's Yeast

Brewer's yeast (also known as "nutritional yeast" and "primary yeast") contains almost no fat and is low in calories, yet it contributes a great deal to our diet. Among other assets, it is an excellent source of the B vitamins and is an inexpensive source of protein; it contains sixteen amino acids found in protein. It also contains eighteen important minerals. It comes in powder form and can be added to soups, sauces, salad dressings, fruit juices and milk drinks, stews, and meat loaves. It may be used in baking, and it blends well with peanut butter. It lends itself best to dishes with a strong flavor because its own flavor is pronounced. Start using brewer's yeast by the teaspoonful. Many people take at least one tablespoon a day and some take several tablespoons a day for their general health.

Nonfat Dry Milk

Nonfat dry milk is one of the most convenient ways to add nutrition to your meals because it may be incorporated into almost any dish, drink, casserole, baked goods, or other food. Its protein value is high, and it should be included in all protein drinks for fortification. Use the noninstant type; the instant type has gone through more processing and is, therefore, stripped of more nutrients.

Soybean Products

The carbohydrate content of the soybean is low and the protein value is high. Soybeans are especially rich in calcium, phosphorus, and iron and contain a number of vitamins; some soybean products contain A, B, and C, while the oil has vitamins A and D and is a good source of vitamins E, "F" (actually a group of fat constituents known as unsaturated fatty acids), and K. Soybeans are rich in lecithin which is important to every living cell in the body.

Soybean products come in many forms and thus are practical for frequent use. The products are flour, milk, grits, sprouts, and the beans themselves, which may be used green, dry, or roasted. Roasted soybeans may be used like any nut and should be kept on hand for snacks and to add to cereals, salads, desserts, casseroles, and other foods.

Lecithin

Lecithin used to be extracted mostly from egg yolks but is now manufactured in large quantities from soybeans. Lecithin serves an essential function in the body because it is nature's cholesterol emulsifier. That is why we may be happy that eggs, which are so good for us, are rich in lecithin as well as other important nutrients. When oils are refined and hydrogenated (the usual practice today), the valuable natural lecithin in them is discarded.

Lecithin comes in powder form, in granules, and in capsules. It may be added to almost any drink and to many dishes.

Wheat Germ

Wheat germ is the heart of the wheat; it is a concentration of valuable nutrients and is the reason that bread was called "the staff of life." Wheat germ has protein value and is an excellent source of vitamin E, B complex, and phosphorus. It is the part of the wheat that industry removes from flour to keep the flour from spoiling on the shelves. We are the poorer by far for its having been stripped from so much of our food supply. It is, therefore, most important to add wheat germ everywhere we can. Buy it fresh and keep it refrigerated.

Wheat germ has a nutlike flavor, an interesting texture, and a great deal of nutrition. Sprinkle it on cereals, salads, fruits, ice cream, and puddings; use it in baking and cooking; use it in soups and sauces; blend it in drinks; mix it with peanut butter for sandwiches; and use it for "breading," either by itself or mixed with whole-grain bread crumbs for coating food to be sauteed and topping casseroles to be baked.

Rice Polish

Like wheat germ, rice polish is a concentration of nutrients stripped by man from natural rice: brown rice. Brown rice has sustained people for generations in many parts of the world, but when polished rice came onto the market, the disease beriberi became prevalent among those whose diet consisted largely of rice. Interestingly enough, the cure for beriberi is rice polish. We cannot improve upon God's formula for the health imparted by healthful foods. Rice polish is rich in vitamin B and minerals. Use it often. It may be used in baking, in sauces, and sprinkled on or cooked in cereals. It may be added to healthful drinks, casseroles, meat loaves, and many other dishes.

Yogurt

Bran Flakes

We are hearing more today about the important role bran plays in the proper functioning of our systems and that bran is the key to many of our civilized diseases. Nutritionists have known this for the forty years I have been listening to them, and I rejoice that now the medical profession is accepting this basic fact. As a result, many people are being told to eat bran. However, there are different kinds of bran cereals, some of which allude to being entirely bran but are not. Read labels to find what is in the product; there may be sugar and other additives.

Buy unprocessed bran flakes at the natural food stores, which have been specializing for many years in the products the food industry has been stripping from our foods.

Bran flakes may be eaten alone as a cereal, or they may be sprinkled on other cereals. They may be used in baking, in health drinks, in vegetable casseroles, and in ground meat dishes.

Rolled Oats

Rolled oats have good protein value and make a nutritious breakfast either in granola or in oatmeal. However, they may also be used in all kinds of baked goods, pancakes, and confections. And they may be used in place of bread crumbs as a binder in meat and fish mixtures. Buy the old-fashioned kind, not the quick version; every process robs natural foods of more valuable nutrients.

Yogurt

Yogurt has been used since biblical times in many countries and through the ages has been considered an important therapeutic agent. Today it has been found valuable in offsetting the frequent side effects of antibiotic therapy because it restores the normal flora of the intestines while, at the same time, inhibiting undesirable organisms. It aids digestion, and the acid content helps calcium to be better assimilated. Furthermore, yogurt aids the body in its own manufacture of B vitamins so essential to the health of the nervous system.

Yogurt is easily made at home:

Heat 1 quart milk (whole or skimmed) to lukewarm (100°, or until it bites your little finger slightly at the count of 10).

Remove from heat and stir in 2 tablespoons of your last batch of yogurt (or a package of starter obtained at a natural food store).

Pour into a glass bowl or crock with lid and wrap immediately in a bath towel and set in a warm place for 8 to 10 hours.

If you purchase yogurt at the supermarket, be sure to read the labels. Do not buy yogurt with additives (with the exception of the little gelatin or carrageenin needed to keep yogurt stable in shipping). Do not buy the yogurt containing fruit and sugar. Add your own fruit to plain yogurt.

Yogurt is a great addition to many dishes; it is also excellent eaten by itself with a little fresh fruit or applesauce and nutmeg. Use it in place of sour cream where you wish; use it in combination with mayonnaise or by itself as a salad dressing; use it in fruit and milk drinks, in baking, and to tenderize meat. It adds an interesting flavor to ground beef and ground lamb and makes a splendid marinade for chicken and fish.

Carob Powder

Carob powder will be indispensable to those who are rearing children. Our children were brought up on carob brownies, carob puddings, carob drinks, and carob ice cream as their cherished treats. It may be substituted for cholcolate in any recipe:

> 3 tablespoons carob powder dissolved in
> 2 tablespoons water equals 1 square
> (1 ounce) chocolate,

and it may be used in the same proportions as cocoa.

Carob powder, like yogurt, dates back to biblical days. Its most popular name is "St. John's Bread" because it is believed to be the food which sustained John the Baptist during his days in the wilderness. The carob tree is of the locust family and is sweet like honey; its natural sugars run approximately 46 percent. The Israelites called it "boekskur," or "God's bread"; the Romans referred to it as "carobi," meaning "bread from the tree" because it sustained life; and the British named it "honey locust."

Carob powder has a number of advantages over chocolate: it has more protein, less fat, less carbohydrates, and fewer calories, and it is a properly balanced alkaline food which is readily digested. It does, however, have a high natural sugar content, so, like honey, this should be taken into account by those on sugar-free diets.

Nuts and Nut Butters

Nuts and nut butters have good protein value and contain both vitamins and minerals. Furthermore, they are of a texture important to a good diet. Their uses are innumerable. Nuts should be kept on hand at all times for snacks, lunch pails and brown bags, refreshments, and to add to many dishes. They are an asset to almost everything, including breakfast cereals, baked goods, salads, all kinds of lunch and dinner dishes, and desserts. And nut butters cannot be surpassed for use in sandwiches and cookies. Buy 100-percent peanut butter. The variety in the supermarket, for the most part, is made of only 90-percent peanut butter (now required by law after a long struggle in Washington against the peanut butter manufacturers who used few peanuts and large percentages of fat), emulsifiers to keep the oil mixed, sugar, and hydrogenated oil, which is a nutrient-altering and -robbing process. Read labels before you buy nut butters, or buy those ground fresh before your eyes.

Mung Beans & Sprouts

Seeds and Sprouting Seeds

Seeds and sprouts are valuable foods. This is easy to understand when we consider that seeds hold the secret of life; they perpetuate life and, therefore, contain nearly every single food element known to man as well as holding all the elements not yet discovered by man. They are a living food, which makes them a perfect food. Seeds have splendid protein, mineral, and vitamin value essential to mental and physical health. Besides all this, they are delicious; they are easy to keep on hand, and they complement innumerable drinks, breakfast, lunch, and dinner dishes, soups, salads, and desserts. The recipes in this book attest to that.

So, keep a supply on hand at all times and toss a handful of seeds or sprouts into your food whenever you can.

Sprouts are easily grown at home (see page 197), and you can have two or three kinds on hand at all times.

Herbs

Herbs are flowers, leaves, fruits, seeds, roots, barks, and mosses, and their quality is high. Herbs are intrinsic to many famous and favorite dishes the world over, and they have been credited with therapeutic value through the ages. Of importance to the organically minded is the fact that almost nowhere in the world are herbs artificially sprayed or fertilized. Natural food enthusiasts enjoy experimenting with herbs.

Seasonings

There are other seasonings besides herbs and spices to enhance our cooking, and some of them add good nutrition as well. Among these seasonings are:

Kelp and dulse are seaweeds, rich in vitamins, minerals, and trace minerals. They come in granule and powder form and may be used on and in our foods like salt and pepper.

Vegetable salts come in several brands and lend slightly different flavors. They are high in minerals and other food factors which make them healthful seasonings and good substitutes for regular table salt, especially for those on sodium-free diets.

Garlic is a member of the onion family. It has meant more to people through the ages than just a food with valuable aromatic and flavor-enhancing properties; it has been credited with medicinal properties as well. In any case, garlic can be used more freely than it is, and its careful use produces truly gastronomical results.

Sea salt is produced by the evaporation of sea water and is preferred because of its abundance of trace minerals. Any salt, however, should be used with restraint.

Pecan Nuts

Egg

Corn Meal

Breakfast and Brunches

Fish

Mushrooms

Grapefruit

Cottage Cheese

Oats

Onion

Doctors and nutritionists tell us that breakfast is the most important meal of the day; we are fueling the furnace to meet the morning's demands. Tests show that children who go to school without a good breakfast do not function as well as those who have eaten breakfast, and that the contrast between those who are properly nourished and those who aren't is striking.

It is lamentable that the public is bombarded with millions of dollars worth of misleading advertisements on cereals, one of our staples. The majority of packaged cereals are made of refined flours and contain a high percentage of sugar and some additives. You will note that those that boast of having some synthetic vitamins and one or two minerals list sugar as one of the first ingredients; ingredients are listed according to their predominance. In order to obtain all the many vitamins, minerals, trace minerals, as well as the elements not yet discovered in whole grains, avoid processed cereals and, at the same time, spare yourself the sugar and additives.

Cured meats are not included in my recipes because of their additives, mainly the nitrates and nitrites. I have included bacon a few times, however, because it is now obtainable without additives in certain parts of the country. Frankfurters are also now made without additives. Ask your natural food store for these items.

General Information on Grains

Make your own blend of cereals with whole or cracked grains. Whole grains are cooked in 2 to 3 times as much water as grain and may be slowly simmered, baked in an oven, or cooked in an electric slow cooker. Whole grains may be used separately or may be combined in any proportion desired. Use whole wheat, whole rye, triticale, barley, buckwheat, oats, brown rice, millet, soy grits, or corn meal. They may be seasoned with sea salt or tamari soy sauce, and dried fruit such as raisins may be added. They may be served with fresh fruit or a little honey, molasses, or pure maple syrup.

Cracked, flaked, and ground grains may also be mixed as desired. They cook more quickly than whole grains. They require 2 to 3 times the amount of water or milk as grain and should be cooked 25 to 30 minutes. Cracked grains may also be prepared the night before by adding 1 part grain to 3 parts boiling water and allowing the water to come to a boil again, then covering and allowing the cereal to stand overnight. It may be reheated in the morning, or it may be left in a warm oven overnight. Seeds, nuts, and dried fruit may be cooked with the cereals. Wheat germ, bran flakes, or rice polishings may be added with a little liquid at the end of the cooking period.

Bulgur (Cracked Wheat) Cereal

1 tablespoon oil
1 cup bulgur
¼ cup sesame seeds
¼ cup chopped nuts
3 cups water or milk
¼ teaspoon sea salt

Sauté the bulgur, seeds, and nuts in the oil until lightly browned.

Cover with water or milk, add salt, and simmer 25 to 30 minutes or until fluffy.
Serves 4

Kasha (Buckwheat Groats) Cereal

1 cup kasha (buckwheat groats)
1 egg, lightly beaten
2½ cups boiling water
2 tablespoons butter
½ teaspoon sea salt

Combine the kasha and egg, and cook the mixture in a dry, heavy pan until the grains are separated. Do not burn. Add the boiling water, butter, and salt, and simmer 25 to 30 minutes or until tender.
Serves 4

Millet Cereal

1 cup whole hulled millet
3 cups water or milk
¼ teaspoon sea salt

Combine all ingredients and simmer, covered, 25 to 30 minutes or until tender.
Serves 4

Cornmeal Mush

5 cups water
1 teaspoon sea salt
1 cup stone-ground corn meal
½ cup grated Cheddar cheese (optional)

Bring water to a boil in the top of a double boiler. Add salt and slowly stir in corn meal. Place over boiling water and cook for 30 minutes. If cheese is used, add it to the mixture for the final 15 minutes of cooking.
Serves 4

Note: For fried cornmeal mush, follow instructions above but with ½ cup more corn meal. When cooked, pour mixture into a lightly oiled 9x9x2-inch pan and refrigerate until firm (or overnight). Cut into strips and saute in butter until lightly brown on both sides. Serve with pure maple syrup, honey, or molasses.

Barley and Onions

2 tablespoons butter
2 tablespoons sesame oil
1½ cups hulled barley
1 onion, chopped
4 cups beef or chicken stock
½ cup burgundy
¼ teaspoon sea salt

Brown barley well in butter mixed with oil.

Add enough water to cover and simmer.

When the water evaporates, add the chopped onion, stock, burgundy, and salt. Put lid on and cook to desired softness,

about 30 minutes. Add water if needed.
Serves 6

Note: Barley must be hulled in order to cook. The whiter the barley, the more pearled it is and the more nutrients have been removed. The barley in natural food stores should be browner than the pearled variety we are accustomed to seeing.

Barley and onions make a good side dish for brunch, luncheon, or dinner. If used for breakfast, omit onion and burgundy. Substitute 4½ cups milk for stock and add 2 to 4 tablespoons wheat germ.

Granola

Make your own granola by experimenting with combinations of ingredients which appeal to you most. Granolas are made of whole-grain flakes, rolled oats, whole-grain flours, seeds, nuts, dried fruits, coconut shreds, and vanilla, honey, or pure maple syrup. Here is one suggestion:

> 5 cups rolled oats or wheat flakes
> 2 cups chopped almonds and walnuts
> 1 cup raw wheat germ
> 1 cup raw natural sunflower seeds
> 2 teaspoons sea salt
> 1 cup corn germ or safflower oil
> ½ cup raw honey or pure maple syrup

Preheat oven to 350°.

Mix all ingredients together in a large bowl. Spread the mixture out in a large, well-oiled baking pan or roaster.

Bake at 350° for 30 minutes. Stir well several times during the baking period and at the end when setting aside to cool.
Makes 10 cups

Variations for Scrambled Eggs and Omelet Fillings

Grated cheese
Diced cooked chicken, chicken livers, kidneys, shrimp,
  fish, bacon, or sausage
Chopped nuts or soybeans
Sliced mushrooms
Herbs: marjoram, sweet basil, tarragon, oregano, pars-
  ley, chives
Chopped ripe olives
Chopped or sliced onions
Capers
Diced avocado
Toasted wheat germ
Sesame, sunflower, or celery seeds
Tomatoes, peeled, seeded, and cut up
Mung bean, alfalfa, or red clover sprouts
Chopped green pepper
Vegetable salt seasoning
Kelp powder
Tamari soy sauce
Worcestershire sauce

Note: Eggs may be cooked in a double boiler. Combine the eggs with desired ingredients in the top of a double boiler and cook over hot water until creamy.

Scrambled Eggs, Spanish Style

½ pound butter
2 medium onions, sliced
3 #2½ cans tomatoes (no additives)
1 tablespoon sea salt
½ teaspoon pepper
½ teaspoon oregano
36 eggs, slightly beaten
1 cup grated Parmesan cheese

Sauté the onion slices in butter until transparent. Add the tomatoes, salt, pepper, and oregano.

Stir in the eggs and cheese, and cook until creamy.
Serves 25

Note: The onions, tomatoes, and seasonings may be combined with the eggs and cheese in the top of a double boiler and cooked over hot water until creamy.

Eggs à la Corrie ten Boom

1 or 2 eggs per serving
2 cherry tomatoes per serving
Butter
Shallow ramekins

Heat the individual shallow ramekins a little in the oven. Melt a little butter in them and drop one or two eggs in each.

Slice the cherry tomatoes, cut each slice in half and place in a circle around the edge of the ramekins. Put a little butter on the yolks to keep them moist.

Either bake or grill four inches from the broiler until set.

Serve immediately.

Note: Eggs may be served in this manner for groups by putting the number of eggs desired in a larger shallow baking dish.

Toast or bacon may be placed in the bottom of each ramekin and the egg dropped on top.

For variation, sprinkle with grated Parmesan cheese.

Eggs With Apples

1 large apple
Brown rice flour
Oil
4 eggs
Sea salt

Peel and core apple; cut into 4 rings. Dredge with flour and sauté on both sides in oil.

Carefully slip an egg on top of each apple ring and sprinkle with salt. Cover and cook until eggs are set.
Serves 4

Tomatoes Stuffed With Scrambled Eggs

2 large, firm, ripe tomatoes
4 eggs
½ teaspoon marjoram
1 tablespoon minced shallots or onion
Dash of sea salt and pepper
1 tablespoon butter
Minced parsley

Preheat oven to 250°.

Cut tomatoes in half and squeeze out the juice and seeds. Remove pulp with sharp knife. Sprinkle the inside with sea salt and drain upside down on a rack in a 250° oven.

Beat eggs with salt, pepper, and marjoram. Melt butter in a skillet and add the shallots or onion; cook slowly just for a moment. Add the eggs and scramble over low heat until creamy curds form. Add sea salt and pepper.

Remove the tomatoes from the oven, place on warm platter, fill them with the scrambled eggs, and sprinkle minced parsley on top.
Serves 4

Baked Eggs With Swiss Cheese

6 slices whole-grain bread cut in rounds
Butter
6 slices Swiss cheese
6 eggs
Sea salt and pepper
¾ cup grated Swiss cheese
½ cup cream or half-and-half

Preheat oven to 350°.

Sauté bread rounds on one side in butter and arrange brown side up in a buttered baking dish.

Place a slice of Swiss cheese on each round and carefully slip an egg on top of cheese. Sprinkle with salt, pepper, and grated Swiss cheese.

Pour cream around eggs and bake at 350° about 10 minutes or until eggs are set.
Serves 6

Austrian Eggs

1 cup sour cream
¼ cup milk
8 eggs
Butter
Chives, chopped

Preheat oven to 350°.

Pour the sour cream and milk into a baking dish.

Carefully slip the eggs into it from a cup one by one. Dot with butter; sprinkle with chopped chives and bake at 350° about 15 minutes or until eggs are set.
Serves 4

Baked Eggs With Shrimp

3 onions, chopped
3 green peppers, chopped
3 tomatoes, peeled and chopped
Unrefined olive oil
Sea salt, pepper, and chili powder
6 large shrimp, shelled and cooked
12 eggs

Preheat oven to 350°.

Sauté onions and green pepper in oil a few moments. Add tomatoes and continue cooking until soft. Season with salt, pepper, and chili powder.

Spoon a little sauce into the bottom of 6 individual baking dishes or ramekins.

Slip 2 eggs into each dish, place a shrimp in the center, and bake at 350° for about 10 minutes or until eggs are set.
Serves 6

Note: This recipe may also be made in one large baking dish. Proceed as with individual dishes.

Mexican Poached Eggs

1 onion, chopped
1 clove garlic, minced
Oil
1 canned, green chili pepper, chopped
2 cups canned tomatoes (without additives)
½ teaspoon sea salt
6 eggs

Sauté onion and garlic in a little oil for a moment. Add the green chili pepper, tomatoes, and salt and simmer.

Poach the eggs in this sauce and serve them in it.
Serves 6

Eggs à la Talleyrand

3 cups cooked whole-wheat, soy, or artichoke spaghetti
6 hard-boiled eggs, sliced
3 tablespoons butter
3 tablespoons oat flour
1 tablespoon nonfat dry milk
½ teaspoon sea salt
¼ teaspoon pepper
1¼ cups warm milk
2 egg yolks
1 tablespoon milk
Grated Parmesan cheese
Paprika

Place warm, cooked spaghetti in a warm serving dish and arrange the sliced eggs on top. Keep warm.

Melt butter, add flour, and simmer 3 minutes. Add dry milk, salt, pepper, and warm milk, stirring. Simmer 5 minutes.

Combine egg yolks with 1 tablespoon milk and add to the sauce.

Pour the sauce over the eggs, sprinkle with Parmesan cheese and a little paprika, and serve.
Serves 6

Fried Eggs With Mushrooms

1 pound mushrooms, sliced
1 tablespoon chopped shallots or onion
1 tablespoon chopped parsley
Butter
8 eggs

Sauté sliced mushrooms, onion, and parsley in butter. Remove from pan and keep warm.

Fry eggs, basting with butter until done.

Serve with mushroom mixture.

Serves 4

Mushrooms and Eggs à la King

1¼ cups butter
2 cups brown rice flour
4½ quarts milk, scalded
1½ pounds mushrooms
¼ cup minced onion
Safflower oil
36 hard-boiled eggs, chopped
2½ cups green pepper, chopped
1½ cups pimiento, chopped
3 tablespoons sea salt
½ teaspoon pepper
50 slices whole-grain toast

Melt butter, add flour, and simmer 3 minutes, stirring. Add scalded milk, stirring vigorously. Simmer 10 minutes.

Sauté the mushrooms and onions in oil and add to the sauce.

Add the chopped eggs, green peppers, pimientos, salt, and pepper to the sauce and keep warm.

Toast bread under broiler and place on warm platters. Pour the mushroom and egg mixture over the toast and serve.

Serves 50

Filet of Fish Meunière

Milk
Brown rice flour
Sea salt
Fish filets
Kelp granules or powder
Safflower oil
Pepper
Lemon juice
Chopped parsley
Butter
Lemon slices

Pour some milk in one deep dish and combine flour with a little salt and kelp in another deep dish.

Dip filets in milk, then in seasoned flour, and sauté in ¼ inch of oil until nicely browned on both sides. Remove the fish to a warm serving dish and sprinkle it with pepper, lemon juice, and chopped parsley. Keep warm.

Pour off oil in pan, and melt in it 1 tablespoon of butter for each piece of fish. Cook until it is a rich brown and pour over the fish. Garnish each filet with a slice of lemon.

Sardines With Vegetables

2 carrots, finely diced
1 pound button onions, sliced
¼ cup green beans, diced
Sea salt, pepper, and kelp powder
Butter
4 tomatoes, peeled, seeded, and chopped
1 sweet green pepper, chopped
2 cans skinless and boneless sardines
1 tablespoon grated Parmesan cheese
Butter

Combine carrots, onions, beans, and seasonings together. Melt butter in a heavy pan and add mixture. Simmer, stirring, 4 or

5 minutes. Add tomatoes and peppers and simmer 2 more minutes.

Spoon the vegetables into the bottom of an oven-proof serving dish and line sardines on top so that they overlap one another a little.

Sprinkle with cheese, dot with butter, and place under broiler until butter and cheese are melted and slightly browned.
Serves 4

Egg Casserole

  6 onions, sliced thin
  Oil
  6 hard-boiled eggs
  Wheat germ
  3 tablespoons butter
  3 tablespoons whole-wheat flour
  1½ cups warm milk
  4 tablespoons grated Gruyere and Parmesan cheeses, mixed
  ½ teaspoon dry mustard
  ½ teaspoon sea salt
  ¼ teaspoon pepper
  Butter

Sauté the onion slices in oil until soft but not browned.

Slice the eggs in thin slices.

Butter a small, narrow, deep baking dish and sprinkle wheat germ on it. Place a layer of onion slices in the bottom, then a layer of egg slices, and repeat until used up.

In a saucepan, melt the butter, add flour, and simmer 3 minutes. Add the milk, stirring, and bring to a boil. Add 3 tablespoons of the cheese, the mustard, salt, and pepper. Simmer 5 minutes.

Pour sauce over contents in dish; sprinkle with remaining cheese and a little wheat germ. Dot with butter and place under broiler until browned.
Serves 4

Codfish Balls

½ pound salt codfish
3 cups raw potatoes, diced
2 eggs, yolks and whites beaten separately
2 tablespoons butter
⅛ teaspoon paprika
¼ teaspoon pepper
Safflower oil

Soak codfish in water overnight.

Dice codfish and potatoes and cook in boiling water until potatoes are tender. Drain.

Beat codfish, potatoes, egg yolks, butter, paprika, and pepper together with an electric beater. Fold in beaten egg whites.

Shape into balls the size of golf balls and fry in hot oil (360°) 2 or 3 minutes until golden brown.

Drain and serve with tomato sauce (page 75)·

Serves 6

Note: The codfish mixture may be formed into cakes, dipped in a mixture of whole-grain flour and wheat germ, and placed on an oiled baking sheet to bake at 375° for 30 minutes.

Codfish Balls

3 pounds salt codfish
10 pounds potatoes, diced
¾ cup butter (1½ sticks)
2½ cups egg yolks, beaten
3¾ cups egg whites, beaten

Soak codfish in water overnight.

Drain codfish and grind. Cook with potatoes in boiling water to cover until potatoes are tender.

Beat codfish and potatoes in electric mixer until fluffy. Add butter, and beaten egg yolks.

Fold beaten egg whites into codfish mixture and form balls with a #8 ice cream scoop. Fry in hot oil (375°) 2 or 3 minutes until golden brown.

Serve with tomato sauce (page 75).
Serves 50

Note: The codfish mixture may be formed into cakes, dipped in a mixture of whole-grain flour and wheat germ, and placed on oiled baking sheets to bake at 375° for 30 minutes.

Fish Cakes

1 cup cooked, flaked, and chopped white fish
3 tablespoons whole-wheat bread crumbs
3 tablespoons wheat germ
1 egg, beaten
½ teaspoon sea salt
½ teaspoon nutmeg
¼ teaspoon pepper
Butter

Combine fish, bread crumbs, wheat germ, egg, salt, nutmeg, pepper. Shape into cakes and sauté on both sides in butter.

Serve with tomato sauce (page 75).
Serves 4

Austrian Sausage Casserole

2 cups diced link sausage (without additives)
2 onions, sliced
Oil
2 tablespoons soy flour
1 cup sour cream
4 green peppers, diced
4 tomatoes, peeled and chopped
½ teaspoon sea salt

Preheat oven to 350°.

Cook sausages in ungreased skillet until browned. Drain well on absorbent paper.

Sauté onions in oil until transparent.

Mix the flour into the sour cream and combine all ingredients. Pour into a buttered casserole and bake at 350° for 30 minutes.
Serves 6

Garbanzo–Sausage Casserole

2 cups garbanzo beans (chick peas)
12 link sausages (without additives)
2 garlic cloves, chopped
1 cup onions, chopped
Unrefined olive oil
½ cup celery, chopped
½ cup carrots, chopped
½ cup tomato paste
3 cups canned tomatoes (without additives)
1 teaspoon oregano
2 tablespoons chopped parsley

Soak garbanzo beans overnight in water to cover.

Preheat oven to 350°.

Cut sausages in half and cook them in an ungreased skillet until brown on all sides. Drain well on absorbent paper.

Sauté garlic and onions in oil for 3 minutes or until transparent.

Combine all ingredients and pour into a casserole dish. Bake at 350° for 2 hours.

Serves 6

Sweet Potato–Sausage Casserole

4 large sweet potatoes
1 pound sausage patties (without additives)
4 apples, peeled and sliced into thick slices
Sea salt
Milk
Honey

Preheat oven to 350°.

Peel and cut sweet potatoes into thin slices. Place half the slices in the bottom of a buttered casserole.

Cook sausage patties in an ungreased skillet until brown on both sides. Drain well on absorbent paper.

Place sausage patties on sweet potatoes in casserole and cover with apple slices. Sprinkle lightly with salt.

Place the remaining sweet potato slices on the apple slices and brush with milk.

Drizzle casserole with honey and bake at 350° for 45 minutes.
Serves 4

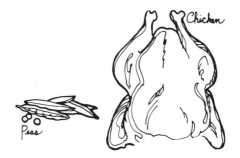

Creamed Chicken or Turkey and Peas

3 tablespoons butter
3 tablespoons brown rice flour
1½ cups milk, warmed
½ teaspoon sea salt
2 cups diced, cooked chicken or turkey
3 pounds or 2 packages frozen peas
2 egg yolks

Melt butter in a saucepan, add flour, and simmer 3 minutes. Add warm milk, stirring until thickened. Add meat and salt, simmer 5 minutes.

Cook peas 5 minutes in minimum amount of water. Puree in blender. Return to pan and keep over heat, stirring, until moisture has evaporated. Stirr in egg yolks and cook a minute or two longer.

Make a border of the pea puree around a warm serving dish and put the creamed chicken or turkey in the center.
Serves 6

West Indian Chicken

2 frying chickens, cut up
Safflower oil
Sea salt and pepper
1 onion, chopped
3 bananas
Wheat germ
Chopped parsley

Preheat oven to 350°.

Sauté chicken in safflower oil until lightly browned.

Place chicken and onion in a buttered casserole dish and sprinkle with salt and pepper. Bake at 350° for 35 minutes.

Peel bananas, cut in quarters, and parboil them 2 minutes.

Lay the bananas on top of the chicken, sprinkle with wheat germ, and bake 10 minutes longer. Garnish with parsley
Serves 6

Baked Lamb Hash

2 tablespoons butter
2 tablespoons whole-wheat flour
1 cup chicken broth, warmed
¼ cup tomato paste
¼ cup water
2 cups diced, cooked lamb
1 onion, chopped
1 clove garlic, minced
Oil
1 tablespoon chopped parsley
½ teaspoon thyme
Sea salt and pepper
Whole-wheat bread crumbs and wheat germ
Grated Parmesan cheese

Preheat oven to 375°.

Melt butter in a saucepan, add flour, and simmer 3 minutes. Add warm chicken broth. Combine tomato paste with water and add to sauce with lamb. Simmer 3 more minutes and set aside.

Sauté onion and garlic in oil until transparent and add to lamb mixture with parsley, thyme, and a dash of salt and pepper.

Pour into a casserole, sprinkle with bread crumbs, wheat germ, and Parmesan cheese. Bake at 375° until bubbly and browned on top.
Serves 6

Liver and Pork Patties

¼ cup onion, chopped
Oil
3 pounds, 6 ounces liver, ground
3 pounds lean pork, ground
1¾ cups whole-grain bread crumbs
1½ cups wheat germ
1 tablespoon sea salt
¼ teaspoon pepper
¾ cup pimiento, chopped
1 green pepper, chopped
½ cup tomato paste
2 eggs, beaten
2 pounds, 4 ounces bacon (50 slices), optional

Preheat oven to 275°.

Sauté onions in oil until transparent.

In a bowl, combine liver, pork, crumbs, wheat germ, salt, and pepper. Add the onion, pimiento, green pepper, tomato paste, and beaten eggs. Mix well.

Form into patties by using a #12 scoop. Encircle with bacon, overlapping by a half-inch, and secure with toothpicks.

Bake at 275° for 45 minutes or until pork is well-cooked.
Serves 50

Liver Smetana

1 pound liver (beef, pork, or lamb)
Sea salt and pepper
Whole-wheat flour
Butter
1 onion, chopped
2 cups sour cream
½ cup chicken broth
2 teaspoons paprika

Wash liver and remove large blood vessel tubes with sharp knife. Sprinkle with salt and pepper, dredge with flour, and sauté briefly in butter. Remove from skillet to a saucepan.

Put onion in skillet with more butter, if needed, and cook until transparent. Add onion to liver in saucepan.

Combine sour cream, broth, and paprika. Pour over liver and onions. Simmer over very low heat a few minutes until heated through.
Serves 4

Note: Kidneys may be prepared the same way.

Liver, Sweetbreads, and Eggs

½ pound calves' liver or beef liver
½ pound sweetbreads
Butter
6 slices whole-grain bread
6 eggs
Butter

Sauté liver and sweetbreads in butter briefly.

Toast bread, divide liver and sweetbreads on top of toast, and place on warm platter in warm oven.

Fry eggs in butter and place one on top of meat on each piece of toast.
Serves 6

Chicken Livers With Apple

1½ pounds chicken livers
Whole-wheat flour
Sea salt
Paprika
Safflower oil
2 onions, sliced and separated into rings
3 tart apples, peeled, cored, and sliced into
    4 slices each
Butter
Honey

Gently wash chicken livers and pat dry. Dredge in flour mixed with a little salt and paprika. Sauté livers until brown on both sides and keep them warm on a warm serving dish.

Sauté onions in oil until transparent and place on top of livers.

Sauté apple rings in butter, spread a little honey on the tops, and arrange on top of liver and onions.
Serves 6

Pineapple

Chicken Livers With Pineapple

1½ pounds chicken livers
Tamari soy sauce
Peanut oil
1 cup pineapple chunks
1 cup slivered almonds
3 tablespoons cornstarch
2 cups pineapple juice

Marinate chicken livers in tamari sauce for 5 minutes, and sauté briefly in oil. Add the pineapple chunks and almonds to the pan and cook, stirring, for a few minutes.

In a separate pan stir cornstarch into a little of the pineapple juice. Place on heat and add remaining juice, stirring until thickened.

Pour the pineapple sauce over the chicken liver mixture.

Serve with whole-grain toast, whole-grain English muffins, or cooked brown rice.

Serves 6

Pancakes and Waffles

In making pancakes and waffles, you may use any recipe you like, whether it makes thin pancakes of flour, eggs, and milk (no baking powder or yeast), or thicker pancakes with the addition of baking powder, or raised pancakes made with yeast. The object in cooking nutritionally is to use whole-grain flours instead of refined flours and to use honey or un-sulphured molasses instead of sugar when a recipe calls for sweetening.

Flours may be used or combined in any proportions you wish. One example would be ¾ cup whole wheat, buckwheat, or triticale, combined with ½ cup whole rye, ½ cup corn meal, and ¼ cup soy flour. Such a combination totaling 2 cups of flour may be combined with 2 or 3 eggs, ½ teaspoon sea salt, and 1½ cups of milk, or as much milk as desired for consistency of pancake.

In making waffles, particularly, it is best to separate the eggs and beat them. Add the beaten egg yolks to the pancake mixture and fold the beaten whites in last.

Serve pancakes and waffles with pure maple syrup, raw honey, or fruit sauces.

Fruit sauces may be made from any fruit: strawberries, blueberries, plums, apricots, and so forth. Cook them until soft. Then blend in an electric blender until smooth and return to stove. Cook down until thick. If too tart, a little honey may be added.

Chopped nuts, seeds, and berries may also be added to pancake and waffle batters. Adding a half cup or so will not alter the recipe; if the consistency is too thick, more liquid may always be added at the end. It is advisable to coat the nuts and berries with a little flour before adding to batter so they will remain dispersed throughout the batter, and add them last.

Pancake and waffle batters may be enriched further with the addition of nutritional yeast, wheat germ, rice polishings, nonfat dry milk, and kelp, dulse, or other powdered seaweed.

Peanut Butter Pancakes

1 egg
¼ cup butter, melted
¼ cup 100 percent peanut butter
1 cup whole-wheat flour
½ teaspoon sea salt
1 cup milk

Beat egg until light, then beat in butter and peanut butter.

Mix flour and salt and add in thirds alternately with milk to the egg mixture.

Pour by large spoonfuls onto lightly oiled hot griddle or skillet. Cook until bubbles form on the surface and edges become dry. Turn and bake on other side until lightly browned, about 2 minutes.
Serves 4

Cottage Cheese Pancakes

2 eggs, beaten
1 cup cottage cheese
3 tablespoons wheat germ
3 tablespoons whole-wheat or brown rice flour
1 tablespoon melted butter

Combine all ingredients and cook on oiled griddle until browned on both sides.
Serves 2–3

Rolled Oat Pancakes

½ cup whole-wheat pastry flour
4 teaspoons baking powder
1 teaspoon sea salt
1½ cups rolled oats
¼ cup protein powder
1 tablespoon bran
1 teaspoon cinnamon
3 eggs, slightly beaten
2 tablespoons oil (1 tablespoon peanut oil, 1 tablespoon all-blend oil)
1 teaspoon unsulphured molasses
¾ cup water
¾ cup milk

Sift together flour, baking powder, and salt. Stir in the remaining dry ingredients.

Combine liquid ingredients.

Combine liquid and dry ingredients, mixing well.

Pour by large spoonfuls onto a lightly oiled hot griddle and bake until brown on both sides.

Serve with fruit sauce (page 57).

Serves 6

Hanukkah Potato Pancakes

2 raw potatoes, cut into small cubes or grated
1 onion, chopped or grated
Sea salt and pepper
¼ teaspoon baking powder
1 egg, slightly beaten
1 tablespoon whole-wheat flour
Safflower oil

Combine all ingredients and drop by tablespoon into hot oil; brown on both sides.

Serve with sour cream and applesauce.

Serves 2

Eggs

Soy Pancakes

4 eggs, yolks and whites beaten separately
1½ cups milk
1 teaspoon sea salt
2 cups soy flour

Combine egg yolks, milk, and salt. Stir in flour, fold in beaten egg whites and drop by spoonfuls on warm, oiled griddle. Brown on both sides.
Serves 4–6

Note: Add more milk for thinner batter. Soy flour browns very quickly; therefore, the griddle must not be too hot.

Danish Sour Cream Waffles

1 cup whole-wheat flour
1 teaspoon baking powder
1 teaspoon ground cardamon
½ teaspoon sea salt
2 eggs, yolks and whites beaten separately
4 tablespoons butter, melted
1 cup sour cream
1 cup buttermilk
1 tablespoon honey

Combine flour, baking powder, cardamon, and salt in a bowl.

To the beaten egg yolks, add the melted butter, sour cream, buttermilk, and honey, blending well.

Add liquid ingredients to dry ingredients and fold in beaten egg whites.

Bake in hot, oiled waffle iron.
Serves 6

Raised Whole-Wheat Pancakes

1 tablespoon dry yeast
1½ cups lukewarm milk
1 tablespoon unsulphured molasses
2 eggs, lightly beaten
2 tablespoons oil
1 cup whole-wheat flour
¼ cup wheat germ
¼ cup nonfat dry milk

Dissolve yeast in lukewarm milk.

Add the remaining ingredients and drop by spoonfuls onto hot, oiled griddle. Cook until bubbles form, then turn to brown the other side.
Serves 4–6

Cantaloupe

Whole-Grain Waffles With Yeast

1 tablespoon dry yeast
1 cup lukewarm milk
4 eggs, beaten
3 tablespoons oil
½ teaspoon sea salt
2 cups whole-grain flour or blend of flours

In a bowl dissolve yeast in lukewarm milk.

Combine eggs, oil, and salt; stir into milk.

Stir flour into liquid, blending well. Set aside in a warm place until the mixture starts to bubble.
Bake in a hot, oiled waffle iron.
Serves 4–6

Note: 2 to 4 tablespoons honey may be added to batter if a sweet waffle is desired.

French Toast

2 eggs, slightly beaten
⅔ cup milk
½ teaspoon salt
6 thick slices day-old whole-grain bread
Butter
Cinnamon
Honey

Combine eggs, milk, and salt. Soak bread in this mixture a minute or two and sauté in butter until brown on both sides. Or place on a buttered baking sheet and brown on both sides under broiler.

Sprinkle with cinnamon and drizzle with honey.
Serves 6

Note: ¼ teaspoon cinnamon may be added to the milk-and-egg mixture.

Grated cheese may be sprinkled on the French toast; put toast back under the broiler for a moment to melt cheese.

Baked Bananas

6 bananas, ripe but not flecked with brown
6 teaspoons butter
6 teaspoons wheat germ
6 teaspoons honey

Preheat oven to 350°.

Wash bananas and place them in their skins on a baking pan. Slit each one lengthwise almost to the bottom skin.

Make a paste of the butter, wheat germ, and honey and force 3 teaspoons of the mixture into each slit.

Bake at 350° for 20 minutes.
Serves 6

Oranges

Cheddar
Cheese

Radishes

Lunches

Spinach

Acorn
Squash

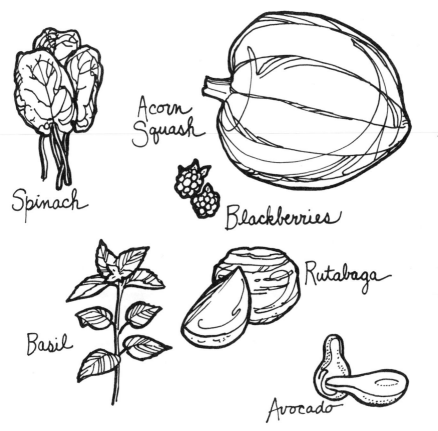

Blackberries

Basil

Rutabaga

Avocado

Lunch is a meal which too many of us neglect. We do not take into consideration the nutritional complement and balance our bodies require to function at top efficiency. Some of us reach for a sandwich of thick, refined bread and a piece of pie; others of us settle for a "slimming" salad accompanied by neither protein nor carbohydrates; and our children gorge themselves on a variety of nonnutritious foods, such as French fries, pop, and candy.

The following recipes are given to encourage the use of nutritious foods and to present a variety of luncheon dishes. Sometimes we have the right balance of food category-wise, but we succumb to the wrong foods within those categories. I include a number of recipes for organ meats and fish because they are too often overlooked and are extremely important to a good diet.

When a recipe for a luncheon dish does not include a green vegetable, fruit, and protein or wholesome carbohydrate (such as whole grains), be sure to round out the menu with whatever is missing.

Besides the luncheon dishes listed in this chapter, there are numerous sandwich suggestions in the chapter "Lunch Pails and Brown Bags," and many soups and salads in the chapters on those categories. The combinations of soups, salads, and sandwiches with the addition of fruit are infinite and make a happy balance for nutritious lunches.

Flounder Tarragon

6 filets of flounder
Butter
1 cup drained, canned tomatoes (without additives)
1 garlic clove, minced
½ teaspoon tarragon

Brown the fish on both sides in foaming butter and remove to a warm platter.

Place the tomatoes, garlic, and tarragon in a saucepan and simmer together a few minutes until heated through; then pour over the fish.
Serves 6

Crab Meat Mold

2 teaspoons gelatin
¼ cup water
½ cup mayonnaise
2 cups crab meat
1 cup celery, chopped fine
1 tablespoon chopped chives
¼ teaspoon tarragon
½ teaspoon kelp granules or powder
3 hard-boiled eggs
Watercress or parsley
Black olives

Soak gelatin in water for 5 minutes and dissolve in top of double boiler over hot water. Stir it into the mayonnaise.

Combine crab meat, celery, chives, tarragon, and kelp, and combine with mayonnaise mixture.

Rinse a quart mold with cold water and pour the crab meat mixture into it. Refrigerate until firm.

Unmold on a bed of lettuce and garnish with quartered hard-boiled eggs, sprigs of watercress or parsley, and black olives.
Serves 6

French Filet of Sole

6 sole filets or other white fish
¼ cup slivered almonds or sesame seeds
Butter
Lemon wedges
Chopped parsley

Brown the fish on both sides in a generous amount of foaming butter and remove to a warm platter.

In the same skillet, brown the almond slivers or sesame seeds and pour over the fish.

Dip lemon wedges in chopped parsley and garnish platter with them.
Serves 6

Deviled Tuna

½ cup milk
1 small onion, chopped fine
1 teaspoon sea salt
½ teaspoon kelp granules or powder
⅛ teaspoon cayenne
½ teaspoon mustard powder
2 teaspoons Worcestershire sauce
¼ teaspoon marjoram
¼ teaspoon thyme
1½ cups water-packed tuna, drained and flaked
Wheat germ
Parmesan cheese, grated

In a saucepan, combine milk, onion, salt, kelp, cayenne, mustard powder, Worcestershire sauce, marjoram, thyme, and tuna. Heat through until it simmers.

Pour into 4 warmed ramekins and sprinkle with wheat germ and Parmesan cheese.

Place under broiler and brown lightly.
Serves 4

Tuna–Noodle Casserole

4 cups cooked noodles (whole-wheat, soy, or artichoke)
1 onion, chopped
Oil
2 7-ounce cans water-packed tuna, drained
5 tablespoons butter
4 tablespoons brown rice flour
1 tablespoon soy flour
1 tablespoon nonfat skim milk powder
1½ cups hot milk
1 teaspoon sea salt
¼ teaspoon garlic powder
½ teaspoon celery seed
1½ cups natural, white Cheddar cheese, grated

Preheat oven to 375°.

Cover bottom of casserole with ⅓ of the noodles.

Sauté onion in a little oil until transparent and combine with tuna.

Melt butter in saucepan, add flours and powdered milk, simmering 3 minutes. Add hot milk, gradually, stirring until smooth and thickened. Add salt, garlic powder, celery seed, and 1 cup of the cheese. Stir and simmer another moment.

Place half of the tuna over the noodles in the casserole and pour half of the sauce over the tuna.

Spread half of the remaining noodles over the tuna and add remaining tuna on top of noodles. Pour over the remaining sauce.

Place the remaining noodles on top of the second layer of tuna and sprinkle with the remaining cheese.

Bake at 375° for 45 minutes.

Serves 6–8

Japanese Filet of Sole

1 cup tamari sauce
½ teaspoon powdered ginger
1 tablespoon honey
6 sole filets or other white fish
Peanut or sesame oil

Mix the soy sauce, ginger, and honey. Marinate the fish in this mixture for one hour.

Remove the fish from the marinade and brown in oil.

Serves 6

Seafood Newburg

1 cup mushrooms, sliced
Oil
2 tablespoons butter
1 tablespoon brown rice flour
1 cup hot cream or half-and-half
½ teaspoon sea salt
⅛ teaspoon cayenne
2 egg yolks, well-beaten
2 tablespoons dry sherry
3 cups seafood
6 slices whole-grain bread

Sauté mushrooms in a little oil and set aside.

Melt butter in top of a double boiler over direct heat. Add flour and simmer 3 minutes. Add hot cream, stirring. Do not boil.

Place pan over hot water (in bottom of double boiler) and add the salt, cayenne, and beaten egg yolks, stirring for 3 minutes. Add sherry, seafood, and mushrooms, and allow to heat through well.

Toast bread and cut in half diagonally. Place on warm platter; pour Seafood Newburg over the toast and serve.
Serves 6

Baked Halibut With Herbs

¼ cup sesame oil
¼ cup lemon juice
½ teaspoon sea salt
½ teaspoon kelp granules or powder
½ teaspoon paprika
6 halibut steaks
½ cup onion, chopped
1 teaspoon thyme
1 teaspoon basil
1 teaspoon marjoram
Lemon wedges
Parsley

Combine oil, lemon juice, salt, kelp, and paprika in a bowl. Place fish in a buttered shallow baking dish and pour mixture over fish. Allow fish to marinate for one hour.

Preheat oven to 450°.

Sprinkle the fish with onion and herbs and bake at 450° for 10 minutes or until done; the fish will flake easily when done.

Serve with lemon wedges and sprigs of fresh parsley.
Serves 6

Salmon Cakes With Mushroom Sauce

2 cups canned salmon, flaked
½ cup whole-wheat bread crumbs
2 eggs, beaten
½ teaspoon sea salt
½ teaspoon kelp granules or powder
⅛ teaspoon paprika
Butter

Combine all ingredients except butter and form into cakes.

Sauté salmon cakes in butter until brown on both sides. Serve with Mushroom Sauce.

Mushroom Sauce

¼ pound fresh mushrooms, cleaned and sliced
1 cup water
2 tablespoons butter
2 tablespoons brown rice flour
¼ teaspoon sea salt

Simmer mushrooms in water for 3 minutes. Drain, reserving liquid.

Melt butter in saucepan, add flour and simmer 3 minutes. Add mushroom liquid, stirring until smooth and thickened. Stir in salt. Add mushrooms and simmer 5 minutes.

Serves 6

Salmon–Celery Loaf

8 pounds cooked, flaked salmon
2½ pounds soft whole-wheat bread crumbs
½ cup nonfat powdered skim milk
1¾ pounds celery, diced fine
4 tablespoons chopped onions
½ pound butter
2½ tablespoons sea salt
2 tablespoons kelp granules or powder
2⅔ quarts milk
11 eggs

Preheat oven to 350°.

Combine salmon, crumbs, powdered milk, celery, onions, butter, salt, and kelp.

In a separate bowl combine milk and beaten eggs; add to salmon mixture and mix thoroughly.

Pour into 6 well-buttered or oiled 9" x 5" loaf pans and bake at 350° for 40 minutes.
Serves 50–55

Salmon Loaf

1 1-pound can salmon, drained and flaked
2 cups soft whole-wheat bread crumbs
1 tablespoon onion, chopped fine
2 tablespoons nonfat powdered skim milk
2 tablespoons melted butter
½ teaspoon sea salt
½ teaspoon kelp granules or powder
½ cup milk
1 egg, slightly beaten
2 pounds or 1 package frozen peas
Sauce

Preheat oven to 350°.

Combine salmon, crumbs, onion, powdered milk, butter, salt, and kelp.

In a separate bowl combine milk and egg; add to salmon mixture and mix thoroughly.

Shape into a loaf in buttered shallow baking pan or loaf pan. Bake at 350° for 40 minutes. When loaf is almost done, prepare sauce and peas.

Sauce

> 2 tablespoons butter
> 2 tablespoons onion, chopped
> 2 tablespoons whole-wheat flour
> ½ teaspoon mustard powder
> ½ teaspoon sea salt
> ¼ teaspoon pepper
> 1 cup milk, warmed

Melt butter in saucepan, add onion, and cook until transparent, not browned. Add flour and simmer 3 minutes.

Stir in mustard, salt, and pepper. Gradually stir in the warm milk and cook until smooth and thickened.

Steam peas over hot water for 4 or 5 minutes and surround the salmon loaf with them on warm platter.

Serve the sauce with salmon loaf and peas.

Serves 3–4

Fish

Salmon Soufflé

3 tablespoons butter
3 tablespoons brown rice flour
1 cup milk, warmed
½ teaspoon sea salt
½ teaspoon kelp granules or powder
1¼ cups flaked, cooked salmon
3 egg yolks, beaten
3 egg whites, beaten (4 whites if eggs are small)

Preheat oven to 375°.

Melt butter in saucepan and add flour. Simmer 3 minutes. Add milk, gradually, stirring until thickened. Add salt, kelp, and salmon.

Fold beaten egg yolks into salmon mixture.

Beat whites until stiff and fold into mixture.

Butter a 1-quart soufflé dish and gently spoon mixture into it. Bake at 375° for 20 to 25 minutes. Serve at once.

Serves 4–6

Creamed Sweetbreads and Chicken

2 sweetbreads
½ teaspoon sea salt
1 tablespoon lemon juice
2 tablespoons butter
2 tablespoons brown rice flour
1¾ cups hot milk
¼ cup nonfat powdered skim milk
2 tablespoons nutritional yeast
¼ cup cream or half-and-half
1 egg yolk
1 cup cooked chicken, diced
½ cup sliced cooked mushrooms
2 tablespoons dry sherry
6 slices whole-grain bread

Place sweetbreads in a saucepan, cover with water, add salt and lemon juice. Simmer for 15 minutes. Drain and cool. Remove membrane and dice them in large chunks.

Melt butter in saucepan and add flour; simmer 3 minutes. Gradually add hot milk, stirring until smooth and thickened slightly. Add powdered milk and yeast. Simmer 10 minutes.

Mix cream with egg yolk and add to white sauce. Then add chicken, mushrooms, and sherry. Add the sweetbreads carefully, stirring with a fork, so as not to break the fragile sweetbreads.

Toast bread and cut diagonally. Place on warm serving platter. Spoon sweetbread–chicken mixture over toast and serve.
Serves 6

Baked Liver

1 pound liver, sliced
Wheat germ
4 onions, sliced thin
$\frac{1}{2}$ teaspoon thyme
$\frac{1}{2}$ teaspoon nutmeg
1 bay leaf, crumbled
1 teaspoon sea salt
$\frac{1}{4}$ teaspoon freshly ground pepper
$\frac{1}{4}$ cup dry sherry or red wine
Paprika

Preheat oven to 350°.

Combine onions, thyme, nutmeg, bay leaf, salt, and pepper.

Dredge liver in wheat germ and sauté quickly in a little oil.

Oil a baking dish and place the liver in layers with the onion mixture.

Pour wine over contents and sprinkle with paprika. Bake at 350° for 15 minutes.
Serves 4

Variation: Tomato sauce may be substituted for the wine.

Liver and Onions

Wheat germ
½ teaspoon sea salt
1½ pounds beef liver, sliced
Oil
1 teaspoon thyme
1 large sweet onion, sliced thin
1 cup chicken broth

Preheat oven to 350°.

Mix wheat germ and salt. Dredge liver slices in mixture and sauté quickly on both sides in oil, only until brown.

Place the liver in a shallow baking dish and sprinkle with thyme. Separate onion rings and place on top of liver. Cover with broth.

Bake at 350° for 15 or 20 minutes until tender.
Serves 6

Kidney Patties

1 beef kidney, or 4 pork or veal kidneys,
    or 6 pair lamb kidneys
2 teaspoons sweet cider vinegar
¼ cup nonfat skim milk powder
¼ cup wheat germ
¼ cup milk
1 teaspoon sea salt
½ teaspoon kelp granules or powder
1 egg, slightly beaten
Dash Worcestershire sauce
1 leek or onion, chopped
1 garlic clove, minced.

Remove membrane and hard parts from kidneys and chop fine.

In a bowl combine kidneys, vinegar, powdered skim milk, wheat germ, milk, salt, kelp, egg, and Worcestershire sauce.

Lightly sauté onion and garlic in a little butter or oil and add to kidney mixture.

Drop by large spoonfuls onto a skillet or grill brushed with oil; shape with spoon into patties. Brown quickly on both sides.
Serves 6

Soybean–Spinach Loaf

2 cups cooked or canned soybeans
1 cup fresh spinach, chopped
1 cup celery, chopped
½ cup whole-wheat bread crumbs
1 tablespoon onion, minced
1 garlic clove, crushed
½ teaspoon nutmeg

Preheat oven to 350°.

Mash soybeans and mix well with other ingredients.

Pour into an oiled baking dish and bake at 350° for 30 minutes. Serve with Tomato Sauce.

Tomato Sauce

2 cups canned tomatoes
1 onion, chopped
1 garlic clove, minced
1 teaspoon sea salt
2 tablespoons chopped parsley
1 teaspoon sweet basil
1 teaspoon oregano
1 teaspoon thyme
¼ cup safflower oil

Combine in a saucepan and simmer 15 minutes, or cook down to desired thickness.
Serves 4

Soybean Loaf

3 cups green soybeans
½ teaspoon sea salt
¾ cups whole-wheat bread crumbs
2 tablespoons nonfat skim milk powder
3 eggs, slightly beaten
¾ cups soy milk or regular milk
4 tablespoons onions, minced
6 tablespoons unrefined olive oil
¾ teaspoon sea salt
½ teaspoon rosemary
¾ cup tomato juice
1 tablespoon grated lemon peel

Preheat oven to 350°.

Pour boiling water over soybean pods and let stand for a few minutes to ease the shelling. Drain, break crosswise and remove beans from their shells. Cook them in a little boiling water with ½ teaspoon salt, covered, for 20 minutes or until tender.

Mash soybeans and mix well with all the ingredients.

Place in an oiled bread pan and bake at 350° for 30 minutes.
Serves 6

Protein Patties

2 cups cooked lentils
½ cup wheat germ
¾ cup whole-wheat bread crumbs
2 tablespoons soy flour
½ teaspoon sea salt
2 tablespoons minced onion
¼ cup sesame seeds, toasted in a skillet
¼ teaspoon celery seed
Whole-wheat flour
Oil
Ketchup

Mash lentils a little and add wheat germ, bread crumbs, soy

flour, salt, onion, sesame seeds, and celery seeds.

Form the mixture into patties. If too dry, add a little ketchup. Coat lightly with flour and sauté in oil on both sides until browned.

Serve with ketchup.
Makes 8 patties

Cheese Soufflé

3 tablespoons butter
3 tablespoons whole-wheat pastry flour
1 teaspoon soy flour
1 cup milk
$\frac{1}{2}$ teaspoon sea salt
$\frac{1}{8}$ teaspoon cayenne
Pinch of nutmeg
4 egg yolks
5 egg whites
Pinch of sea salt
$\frac{3}{4}$ cup (3 ounces) natural Swiss or
    white Cheddar cheese, grated

Preheat oven to 400°.

Melt butter in saucepan, add flour and simmer, stirring, 3 minutes. Remove from heat and pour in hot milk, stirring vigorously with a wire whisk. Add salt, cayenne, and nutmeg and return to heat for a minute. Then remove from heat.

Whisk egg yolks into white sauce one at a time.

Add pinch of salt to egg whites and beat until stiff.

Stir the grated cheese into the white sauce and carefully fold in the egg whites.

Turn the mixture into a buttered 6-cup soufflé dish and set in the center of the preheated oven. Immediately turn the heat down to 375° and bake for 25 to 30 minutes. Do not open door. It should be firm and nicely browned. Otherwise, bake it about 5 more minutes.
Serves 4

Cheese Dreams

½ cup milk, scalded
1 egg, beaten
¼ teaspoon dry mustard
¼ teaspoon sea salt
¾ pound natural Cheddar cheese, grated
6 slices whole-grain bread

Pour milk into top of double boiler and add egg, mustard, salt, and cheese.

Cook over hot water 15 minutes, stirring every few minutes.

Cool cheese mixture and put in a closed jar in refrigerator until ready for use.

Toast bread slices and spread with cheese mixture. Broil until puffed and lightly browned.
Serves 6

Note: Cheese Dream Sandwiches may be made by spreading the cheese mixture between two slices of bread. Butter the outside lightly and broil until brown on both sides.

Leftover Turkey Casserole

1 onion, chopped
1 cup mushroom pieces
Butter
½ teaspoon sea salt
1 tablespoon paprika
¼ teaspoon nutmeg
8 slices cooked turkey
Cream, half-and-half, or milk
Grated Parmesan cheese
Wheat germ

Preheat oven to 400°.

Cook the onions and mushrooms in a little butter for 5 minutes over low heat; do not let onion brown. Add the salt, paprika, and nutmeg. Spread on the bottom of a casserole.

Mushrooms

Lay the turkey slices on top of the mushrooms and onions. Add enough cream to cover. Sprinkle with grated Parmesan cheese and wheat germ.

Bake at 400° for 10 minutes or until bubbly and brown on top. *Serves 4–6*

Sesame–Almond Baked Chicken

1 cup yogurt
1 egg, beaten
½ cup whole-wheat flour
1 teaspoon salt
6 chicken breasts, skinned and halved
1 cup ground almonds
¼ cup sesame seeds
½ cup wheat germ
Butter
Slivered almonds

Preheat oven to 350°.

Mix yogurt with egg in a bowl.

Combine flour and salt.

Dip chicken breasts in egg-yogurt mixture and then in flour. Place in oiled baking dish.

Mix ground almonds, seeds, and wheat germ together and sprinkle over chicken breasts. Dot with butter.

Bake at 350° for 35 minutes. When done, sprinkle almond slivers over the top and place under broiler for a minute or two to brown.

Avocado With Curried Chicken

¼ cup butter
½ small onion, chopped
1 garlic clove, crushed
1 tablespoon curry powder
4 tablespoons whole-wheat flour
1 tablespoon nonfat skim milk powder
1 cup hot milk
1 cup hot chicken broth
1 teaspoon sea salt
⅛ teaspoon pepper
2 cups cooked chicken, diced
3 large avocados
3 cups cooked brown rice
Peanuts
Chopped hard-boiled egg
Raisins
Coconut

Preheat oven to 350°.

In a saucepan, sauté onion, garlic, and curry powder in butter until onion is cooked, but not brown. Stir in flour and powdered milk; simmer 3 minutes. Add milk and broth, stirring until smooth and thickened.

Add salt, pepper, and chicken. Simmer 10 minutes.

Peel and cut avocados in half.

Spread rice on the bottom of a buttered or oiled baking dish. Arrange avocado halves on rice and heat in 350° oven about 5 minutes.

Remove from oven and spoon hot curried chicken into avocado halves. Serve with bowls of peanuts, chopped hard-boiled eggs, raisins, and coconut.
Serves 6

Scalloped Chicken With Mushrooms

4 cups brown rice
2 gallons water
1 tablespoon sea salt
2 pounds fresh mushrooms, sliced
½ cup ground onions
¾ pound butter
2⅓ cups whole-wheat flour
3 quarts warm chicken stock, milk, or
    half stock–half milk
2¾ pounds uncooked chicken, diced
1½ cups slivered almonds, browned in butter
1½ tablespoons sea salt
2 teaspoons nutmeg
3 teaspoons rosemary
1½ cups raw wheat germ
Butter

Preheat oven to 325°.

Bring rice, water, and 1 tablespoon salt to a boil, covered. Turn heat down and simmer, covered 35 to 40 minutes or until tender. Add more boiling water, if needed.

In a large, heavy pot, sauté mushrooms and onions in butter only until onions are soft, not browned. Blend in flour and add warm stock or milk, stirring vigorously (preferably with large wire whisk), and simmer for 8 minutes.

Stir in chicken pieces, almonds, salt, nutmeg, and rosemary.

Put into 3 shallow 9″ x 15″ baking pans, sprinkle with wheat germ and dot with butter. Bake at 325° for 1 hour.
Serves 50

nutmeg

Indian Chicken Stew

2 chicken breasts, cut in half with skins removed
Yogurt
1 8-ounce can tomatoes
1/2 cup corn kernels
1/2 teaspoon sea salt
1/2 teaspoon ground cumin seed
1 spring onion, sliced thin
1 zucchini, sliced in one-inch slices

Place chicken breasts in heavy pan or slow cooker. Add yogurt to cover, tomatoes, corn, salt, cumin, and onion.

Cook over low heat for 30 minutes, adding zucchini for the last 10 minutes. If slow cooker is used, follow directions for stews with cooker.
Serves 4

Ground Beef Patties Lyonnaise

3/4 cup onion, finely chopped
2 tablespoons butter or oil
1 1/2 pounds lean freshly ground beef
1 teaspoon sea salt
1/8 teaspoon pepper
1/4 teaspoon thyme
1 egg
1/2 cup whole-wheat flour

Cook onions in butter or oil over low heat about 5 minutes until soft but not brown.

Combine the beef, onion, salt, pepper, thyme, and egg, and mix well.

Form into patties and dip in flour, shaking off excess.

Sauté in lightly oiled skillet which is hot enough to sear the meat. Cook about 3 minutes a side, depending upon how rare or well-done you like your patties.
Serves 6

Ground Beef Patties Robert

1½ pounds lean freshly ground beef
2 tablespoons yogurt
1 teaspoon sea salt
½ teaspoon cinnamon
1 teaspoon oregano
½ cup onion, chopped

Combine all ingredients and mix well. Allow mixture to stand, covered, in refrigerator for at least ½ hour.

Form into patties and cook in a little oil in a skillet or on a grill which is hot enough to sear the meat well. Cook 3 minutes a side, depending upon how rare or well-done you like your patties.
Serves 6

Bulgur–Beef Casserole

1½ pounds lean, freshly ground beef
1 small onion, chopped fine
Oil
1 cup bulgur (cracked wheat)
¾ cup boiling water
2 large tomatoes, peeled and chopped
2 tablespoons tomato paste
1 tablespoon nutritional yeast
1 teaspoon sea salt
½ teaspoon basil
½ teaspoon thyme
¼ teaspoon garlic powder

Preheat oven to 325°.

Put meat and onion in a skillet with a little oil; cook, stirring, until meat is gray.

Pour boiling water over bulgur and add to the meat mixture. Combine all ingredients and spoon into an oiled 1½-quart casserole.

Bake at 325° for 1 hour.

Meat Loaf Sandwiches

Cold meat loaf (See page 102)
Butter, softened
Whole-grain bread
Sea salt
Ketchup or mayonnaise
Alfalfa sprouts

Cut meat loaf into ½-inch slices.

Butter slices of bread and place slice of meat loaf on top. Add a little salt and spread with either ketchup or mayonnaise.

Pile alfalfa sprouts on top of the meat, place another slice of bread on top of each and cut into half, diagonally.

Sprouting Seeds

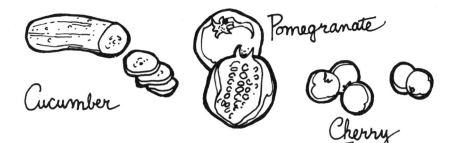

Cucumber

Pomegranate

Cherry Tomatoes

Lunch Pails and Brown Bags

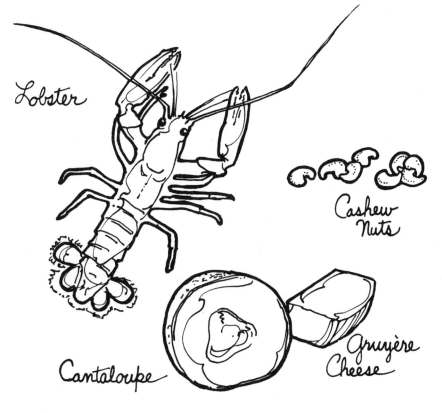

Lobster

Cashew Nuts

Cantaloupe

Gruyère Cheese

Lunch pails have been with us for a long time; brown bags have become a way of life only recently. Both are to be looked upon as an important contribution to increased energy and better health. The lunch pail and the brown bag allow school-children and working men and women to do what is best for their bodies by properly nourishing the cells of those bodies. In so doing, a marked increase in efficiency is the dividend. Numerous studies on the relationship between what we eat, as well as when we eat, and our mental and physical capabilities bear out this statement.

Fixing a lunch to take along to school or work does take some time in the morning. The job may be facilitated, however, with a little organization; and the dividends of a lunch from home go beyond those of better health and mental prowess. The result is that the contents of a lunch pail or brown bag may be consumed leisurely and with utmost enjoyment, while still leaving time for rest, meditation, or exercise—all contributing factors to physical and mental efficiency.

I would make a further suggestion for those who do or do not take lunch to school or to work: take along nutritious snacks. Of almost equal importance to a nutritious lunch is a nutritious snack mid-morning and mid-afternoon. These save the individual from the all-too-common slump most people seem to experience. It was the recognition of this slump that led businesses to give coffee breaks; they found they could count on more productive work from their staffs if they gave them time off for coffee breaks.

Certainly the relaxation aspect of the coffee break is valuable, but energizing the body through proper nourishment is equally valuable; one without the other is half the remedy. In fact, improper nourishment can undo the benefit of whatever rest one attains. The body is not efficiently energized with the stimulating effect that caffeine and sugar bring because a person is lifted only temporarily; he or she then experiences a letdown, at which time the body demands another stimulant. It is well to remember that foods which are too sweet make you crave more sweets because the ensuing rise in blood sugar level occurs as it does with stimulants. Avoid sugar and sugared products; use honey and natural sweeteners, but don't overdo them.

Replace the coffee, roll, or sweet at coffee break time with nutritious snacks that won't let you down at the end of the morning and afternoon—those hours which for many people are a call for more caffeine or a cocktail. Sustaining snacks will maintain your energy level until lunchtime and dinnertime. Many nutritionists agree that it is better to eat less and eat more frequently. Nutritious snacks will result in your eating less at mealtimes.

Do not buy the usual "luncheon" meats—bologna, salami, and various concoctions. These meats are great deceivers. They often consist of inferior grades of meat, considerable fat, dyed red to look like meat, and contain too much salt, to say nothing of a bevy of chemicals you do well to avoid. Slice your own luncheon meats from the good quality meats you have carefully cooked at home.

If bacon or sausage is used, be sure it is a pure product without nitrates, nitrites, and other additives.

The following are a few things for lunch-toters or for those who prepare meals for them:

A pint, squat, wide-mouthed thermos. For hot drinks, first fill with hot water and put the cap on until ready for use. For cold drinks, take the cap off and place in the refrigerator until ready for use.

A strong lunch pail or supply of brown bags. Some people send to mail-order houses for lunch bags imprinted with their initials.

A supply of insulated bags for foods like poultry, seafood, fish, mayonnaise, and dairy products.

A supply of sturdy paper napkins, which can double for placemats if desired.

A jar with a screw-top or a cup-size thermos for cottage cheese and yogurt mixtures, puddings, applesauce, salad, etc.

If you work in an office where you are able to keep a few supplies, it is helpful to have the following on hand:

Strong paper plates

Strong cups (styrofoam or ceramic)
Sharp knife, fork, and spoon
Combination can puncher and bottle opener
Salt and pepper
Carob powder, protein powder or liquid, nonfat dry milk powder, and grain beverages if hot water is available or if you would like to make a cold drink. In the latter case, have a jar with a screw top on hand to use as a shaker.

Avoid artificial sweeteners and imitation dairy products. They contain unnecessary chemicals, and they are not real food.

The lunch pail or brown bag should contain the same balance of nutrition that one would have at home for lunch or dinner. This consists of a good-quality protein—meat, poultry, fish, eggs, or cheese—unrefined carbohydrates such as whole-grain breads and crackers, fresh vegetables, fresh or dried fruit, and a healthful beverage. A wholesome cookie or piece of cake may be included.

Sandwiches

Use whole-grain or sprouted-grain bread such as whole-wheat or whole-wheat sourdough bread, whole-rye bread, soy bread, millet bread, etc., or bread made of a combination of whole-grain flours.

To keep sandwiches fresh, wrap them in wax paper, foil, plastic wrap, or a damp cloth.

Some sandwiches may be prepared early and frozen, but sandwiches with eggs, tomatoes, and mayonnaise (unless mayonnaise is mixed in a spread) do not freeze well.

When including jams, jellies, and relishes in sandwiches, be sure to use those which are made with honey and do not have additives such as artificial color and flavor, preservatives, and the like. Make them yourself or purchase them at natural food stores, but check the labels before buying. Spread a little mayonnaise or butter, not margarine, on the bread. To make your butter easier to spread (and, incidentally, lower in cholesterol), whip ½ cup safflower oil into one pound softened sweet cream butter and scoop it into a jar or crock. It will become firm again in the refrigerator but will soften quickly for spreading.

Use homemade mayonnaise (see chapter 11) or buy mayonnaise made with good vegetable oils and no sugar. These are obtainable in natural food stores.

Use all kinds of lettuce or sprouts in sandwiches. Put a lettuce leaf next to the bread if sliced tomatoes are used to protect the bread from getting soggy.

Combinations for Sandwiches

½ cup ricotta cheese, ¼ cup chopped nuts, 1 chopped celery stalk, and a dash of sea salt.

4 chopped hard-boiled eggs, 1 teaspoon minced onion, 2 tablespoons chopped parsley, ½ teaspoon kelp granules, ¼ teaspoon marjoram, 1 tablespoon lecithin granules, and ⅛ teaspoon salt. Bind with 2 tablespoons mayonnaise mixed with 1 tablespoon yogurt.

½ cup peanut butter mixed with 1 mashed banana, topped with mung bean sprouts. (See page 197.)

Avocado slices, turkey slices, crumbled bacon, tomato slices, and chopped, stuffed olives, moistened with mayonnaise mixed with a little chili sauce.

Flaked tuna fish, chopped celery, chopped onion, sliced avocado, chopped peanuts, mixed with yogurt or mayonnaise, topped with lettuce.

Sliced onion, sliced avocado, sliced Swiss cheese, spread with mustard and mayonnaise, and topped with alfalfa sprouts. (See page 197.)

Sardines with mayonnaise, topped with cottage cheese and chives.

Scrambled eggs, chopped onion, crumbled bacon, and chopped green pepper. Sea salt and pepper to taste.

Kefir cheese with toasted sesame seeds.

All cooked, cold, sliced meats (beef, lamb, liver) or meat loaf, chicken, turkey, fish filets, shrimp, crab, lobster, tuna, salmon, sardines, combined with sliced hard-boiled eggs, cheeses, nuts, roasted soybeans, toasted sesame seeds or sunflower seeds; top with lettuce or sprouts and moisten with mayonnaise, yogurt, sour cream, or a little salad dressing.

Whole pieces of cooked chicken make a nice surprise and change from sandwiches now and then.

Sandwich Spreads

The following are some suggestions; hopefully, they will lead you to devise your own spreads. In so doing, remember to fortify spreads where you can with further nutritious additions, such as, nonfat dry skim milk powder, soy flour, protein powder, lecithin granules or powder, nutritional yeast, nuts, seeds and sprouted seeds, kelp granules or powder, yogurt, and vegetable seasonings (available at natural food stores). The last may be used in place of salt. Make an ample supply of spread at one time and keep it in a jar in the refrigerator or freeze if necessary.

1 pound leftover beef, lamb, liver, meat loaf, chicken, or fish; put in blender with 1 large onion chopped, 3 tablespoons soy flour, ½ cup wheat germ, 2 tablespoons nutritional yeast, 1 teaspoon thyme, and 1 teaspoon curry powder (optional). Moisten with mayonnaise or oil and lemon juice.

1 cup ground cooked liver mixed with 1 tablespoon minced onion, 1 chopped hard-boiled egg, 1 tablespoon chopped parsley, ¼ teaspoon nutmeg or 2 teaspoons chopped pickles, sea salt and pepper to taste, and enough mayonnaise to moisten.

Mix ½ cup minced chicken or flaked tuna, ¼ cup celery chopped fine, 3 ounces cream cheese, kelp powder, sea salt and pepper to taste.

Mix shredded crab meat or lobster with chopped hard-boiled eggs, chopped cucumbers, kelp powder, sea salt and pepper to taste, with a little dry sherry and mayonnaise to moisten.

Combine 1 cup shredded crab meat or lobster, 1 onion chopped, 1 teaspoon celery seeds, 1 cup cottage cheese, ½ cup sprouts, and sea salt to taste. Add a little lemon juice and safflower oil to moisten.

Combine 1 cup flaked, cooked filet of white fish, ¼ cup minced green onions, ½ teaspoon thyme, 1 teaspoon toasted sesame seeds, and enough mayonnaise to moisten.

Combine 12 boneless and skinless sardines with 1 tablespoon minced onion, ½ teaspoon Worcestershire sauce, ½ teaspoon ketchup or tomato sauce, 1 tablespoon chopped stuffed olives, ¼ teaspoon kelp powder, ¼ teaspoon toasted sunflower seeds, and mix with enough mayonnaise or salad dressing to moisten.

Lobster

Blue Cheese

Olives

Onion

Egg Salad Spreads

3 chopped hard-boiled eggs, 1 tablespoon chopped chives, 1 tablespoon chopped stuffed olives, ¼ teaspoon sea salt, ¼ teaspoon paprika, and enough yogurt to moisten.

Combine 3 chopped hard-boiled eggs with ¼ cup soy flour, 1 small carrot chopped, 3 tablespoons chopped green onions, ½ teaspoon marjoram, 2 teaspoons nutritional yeast, and moisten with mayonnaise or salad dressing.

Combine 3 chopped hard-boiled eggs with ¾ cup chopped pecans or almonds, 2 tablespoons chopped, stuffed olives, 1 tablespoon chopped parsley, ¼ teaspoon sea salt, and enough mayonnaise to moisten.

Combine 3 chopped hard-boiled eggs with either minced anchovies, shrimp, or crab meat. Add a little minced celery and enough mayonnaise to moisten. The mayonnaise may be flavored with a dash of Worcestershire sauce to go with the shrimp or crab.

Put in blender 3 hard-boiled eggs, cut up, 1 cup cooked lentils or peas, ¼ cup cottage cheese, 1 tablespoon wheat germ, and 1 teaspoon celery seed. Blend well. If moistening is needed, add a little lemon juice and oil.

Cheese Spreads

Combine 1 cup cottage cheese,* ½ cup cucumber chopped fine, ½ cup celery chopped fine, ½ cup watercress chopped, 1 teaspoon vegetable salt seasoning, pepper, and 1 tablespoon safflower oil with 1 teaspoon lemon juice.

Combine 1 cup cottage cheese with ½ cup chopped walnuts, 1 tablespoon grated onion, and sea salt to taste.

Combine 1 cup cottage cheese with ¼ cup wheat germ, 2 tablespoons nonfat dry milk powder, ¼ teaspoon caraway seeds, ¼ teaspoon celery seeds, 1 tablespoon minced onion, and ½ teaspoon vegetable salt.

Combine 1 cup cottage cheese with ½ cup chopped dried apricots or ½ cup chopped dates, ½ cup chopped walnuts or pecans, and 3 tablespoons lemon juice.

Combine 1 cup cottage cheese with ½ tomato (peeled, seeded, and chopped), 1 tablespoon chopped chives, ½ teaspoon kelp powder, and ½ teaspoon sea salt.

Combine ¼ cup crumbled blue or Roquefort cheese with 1 tablespoon crumbled bacon, ¼ teaspoon dry mustard, 2 teaspoons toasted sesame seeds, and 3 to 4 tablespoons mayonnaise.

Combine 1 cup grated Cheddar cheese with ¼ cup grated carrots, ½ cup chopped green onions, ½ cup tomato sauce, 2 tablespoons nutritional yeast, ½ teaspoon sweet basil, 2 teaspoons toasted sesame seeds, and 1 garlic clove crushed. Blend well and add a little mayonnaise if needed.

Combine 1 pound Swiss cheese grated with ½ cup chopped ripe olives, ½ cup chopped chives, ½ teaspoon crushed caraway seeds (optional), and ¾ cup yogurt or mayonnaise.

Vegetable Spreads

Combine 1 cup chopped cucumber, ¼ cup wheat germ, ¼ cup bran, ½ cup chopped nuts, sea salt to taste, and moisten with salad dressing.

Combine 1 cup shredded cabbage with ¼ cup grated carrots, ¼ cup celery chopped fine, and 1 tablespoon chopped chives. Moisten with yogurt or mayonnaise.

Combine 1 cup shredded green or red cabbage, ¼ cup chopped apples with skins left on, ¼ cup chopped walnuts, 1

*1 cup cottage cheese = ½ pound

teaspoon caraway seeds (optional), and enough mayonnaise to moisten.

Combine 1 cup cooked mashed lentils, soybeans, or navy beans with 1 tablespoon chopped onion, 2 tablespoons chopped celery, 1 tablespoon lemon juice, 1 teaspoon rosemary, and enough mayonnaise to moisten.

Combine ½ cup soy flour with ½ cup 100% peanut butter, 2 tablespoons chopped onions, 1 tablespoon nutritional yeast, and 1 tablespoon chopped parsley. A little honey may be added if desired.

Put in blender 1 cup pitted dates, 1 cup chopped nuts, and ¼ cup orange or pineapple juice or yogurt. If texture is too thin, add soy flour or nonfat dry milk powder.

Combine 2 ripe avocados mashed, ½ pound crumbled bacon, ½ cup chopped cashews, and 2 teaspoons lemon juice. To keep, cover with lemon juice and tight lid.

Combine 2 ripe avocados mashed, 1 garlic clove crushed, 2 tablespoons chopped chives, 2 teaspoons lemon juice, 1 teaspoon grated lemon rind, 1 tablespoon chopped parsley, and sea salt and pepper to taste. A dash of chili powder may be added if desired. To keep, cover with lemon juice and a tight lid.

Combine 1 ripe mashed avocado with 1 banana, 2 tablespoons wheat germ, 2 tablespoons chopped peanuts, and 1 tablespoon lemon juice. To keep, cover with lemon juice and a tight lid.

Combine 1 cup apple butter, or other fruit butter, with ½ cup soy flour, or nonfat dry milk powder, and 3 tablespoons toasted sesame or sunflower seeds.

Nut Butter Spreads

Put in grinder or blender 2 cups peanuts or other nuts, ½ teaspoon sea salt, 1 cup sesame seeds, and ½ cup sunflower seeds. Blend this mixture with enough peanut oil to make it a good spreading consistency. Add a little honey if desired.

Blend together by hand 1 cup 100% peanut butter, ¼ cup

grated carrots, 1 tablespoon chopped celery, and 1 tablespoon raisins. Add a little oil if necessary.

Blend together by hand 1 cup nut butter, 2 tablespoons lemon juice, 1 teaspoon nutritional yeast, and 1 tablespoon chopped dates or figs.

Blend together by hand 1 cup nut butter, ¼ cup chopped green peppers, ¼ cup chopped celery, ¼ cup sprouts, 1 teaspoon toasted sesame seeds, and 2 tablespoons lemon juice.

Suggestions to Fill Out the Lunch Menu

Raw vegetables: carrots, celery, zucchini, small yellow squash, green pepper, broccoli, mushrooms, tomatoes, cauliflower.

Hard-boiled eggs stuffed with variety of seasonings: sea salt, pepper, vegetable salt, curry powder, chili powder, garlic powder, onion powder, herbs, mustard, celery seeds, sesame seeds, kelp powder, or paprika blended with softened butter or mayonnaise.

Natural cheeses, cubed.

To go into cup-size thermoses or containers with tight lids:
  All kinds of salads
  Coleslaw
  Applesauce or other fruit sauces (homemade with honey instead of sugar)
  Yogurt with fresh fruit
  Cottage cheese with chopped tomatoes, fruit, or combinations found under cheese spreads
  Puddings and other desserts

Every lunch pail or bag should contain a piece of fruit if fruit is not already included in the menu. You may be in a position where you can keep a supply of fresh fruit at the office—so much the better.

Beverages to be taken in thermos bottles are listed in the chapters on soups and protein drinks. To these may be added:

Milk
Kefir
Tomato juice and vegetable juices of all kinds
Fruit juices

A delicious protein drink is a great way to give yourself a boost during the day; it will help maintain your energy level. Protein drinks can be carried in a large thermos and can be drunk at lunch and for "coffee" breaks.

Potatoes

Jerusalem Artichoke

Eggplant

Dinners and
Potluck Dishes

Bay Leaf

Chicken

Bananas

Green
Peppers

Broccoli

French
Artichoke

Dinner involves the family; it often involves guests; and sometimes it involves taking a dish to a potluck affair. My chapter on dinner dishes, therefore, offers suggestions for all of these occasions. I also give recipes for quantity cooking so that you will be prepared to produce a dish for a group when called upon.

Dinner gives us a great opportunity to introduce nutritious cooking to our families, our friends, and our Christian gatherings. I believe it is our solemn and joyful responsibility to do so. It is an inescapable fact that it is the consumption of what God provides for our bodies—pure, natural, unadulterated foods —which is to His glory. Hence, partaking of such foods is the Christian's privilege and sets a Christian example.

It is important to remember that dinner should not be a huge meal. Many Americans are given to overeating, and some slimming enthusiasts are apt to make dinner their only meal, which is not wise. Dinner, like lunch, should be a well-balanced meal, but not a larger meal. As previously mentioned, breakfast, lunch, and dinner should be adequate and completely nourishing, but not huge. Small and nutritious snacks between meals may be of great value to some people and will help reduce the tendency of overeating at mealtime.

Remember, too, that whole foods—real foods—are much more satisfying, which means that one may feel replete with smaller portions.

Meatballs With Curried Sauce

1½ pounds freshly ground beef
2 slices whole-grain bread
½ cup milk
1 onion, chopped fine
2 teaspoons sea salt
¼ teaspoon pepper
½ teaspoon nutmeg
1 garlic clove, crushed
3 eggs, beaten
Safflower oil

Soak the bread slices in milk and squeeze out. Break up bread and add to beef.

Sauté the onion in a little oil until transparent.

Combine the meat, onion, seasonings, and beaten eggs. Form into small balls and brown in skillet with as much oil as needed.

Remove the meatballs and make the sauce in the same pan.

Curried Sauce

> 1 onion, chopped fine
> 4 tart apples, peeled, cored, and chopped fine
> 4 tablespoons butter
> 4 tablespoons brown rice flour
> 1 garlic clove, crushed
> 2 tablespoons curry powder
> ¼ cup tomato sauce
> 2 cups beef stock
> 2 tablespoons lemon juice
> ½ teaspoon sea salt

Cook the onions and apples in butter until transparent.

Add the flour, stirring until smooth. Add the remaining ingredients and simmer, stirring, until thickened.

Return the meatballs and the sauce to the pan and heat through.

Serve with brown rice, noodles, or spaghetti (made of whole-wheat, soy, or vegetable flour)

Serves 6

Garlic

Carrots

Spaghetti and Beef

4 large tomatoes
2 teaspoons Worcestershire sauce
3 garlic cloves, crushed
½ teaspoon sea salt
· ½ teaspoon tarragon
½ medium onion, sliced
Butter or oil
1 pound freshly ground beef (half sirloin,
    half round steak)
½ pound whole-wheat spaghetti, cooked

About an hour before serving time, make a tomato sauce as follows:

Cut out the stems of the tomatoes and cut the tomatoes in chunks, leaving skins on (scald and peel if not organically grown).

Place the tomatoes in a large saucepan and cook until soft. Then put in a blender and blend until smooth.

Return to saucepan and add the Worcestershire sauce, garlic, and salt. Sprinkle the tarragon over, leave the lid off, and cook the sauce down over low heat until it is thick.

Sauté the onion slices in a little butter or oil until transparent. Add the ground meat and simmer, stirring frequently. Cook only until the meat starts to turn gray and still has some red in it.

Combine the meat mixture with the tomato sauce and simmer 5 to 10 minutes, stirring frequently.

Serve over hot whole-wheat spaghetti.
Serves 4–6

Beef Ragout

3 pounds lean beef cut into 1½-inch chunks
Whole-wheat flour
Safflower oil
1 zucchini
1 small yellow squash
1 pound green beans
4 to 6 carrots
6 stalks celery
1 onion, chopped
½ cup red wine or dry sherry
1½ teaspoons sea salt
2 crushed bay leaves
Parsley for garnish

Roll beef chunks in flour and brown on all sides in oil.

Wash and cut vegetables in 1-inch pieces.

If an electric slow-cooking pot is used, combine all ingredients and cook for 8 to 10 hours according to instructions on pot.

If the ragout is to be cooked on the stove, combine meat, onion, bay leaves, and wine in a heavy stew pot with a lid. Simmer over very low heat about 1 hour or until tender, adding water if needed.

Then add the vegetables and cook for 6 minutes.

Serve with chopped parsley on top.

Serves 8

Bay Leaf

Beef Goulash With Sour Cream

2 pounds onions, sliced
Safflower oil
8 pounds beef, cut in 1½-inch cubes
1 tablespoon paprika
¼ cup cider vinegar
2 teaspoons caraway seeds
1 teaspoon marjoram
1 tablespoon salt
6 cups beef stock (see page 156)
6 tablespoons butter
6 tablespoons potato flour or whole-wheat flour
2 cups sour cream

In a heavy pot sauté onion slices in oil until transparent.

Add beef cubes and brown them, adding more oil as needed.

Add paprika, vinegar, caraway seeds, marjoram, and salt.

Gradually add the beef stock and simmer over low heat about 1 hour or until tender.

With a slotted spoon, remove beef cubes and set aside.

In a separate pan, melt butter and add flour, stirring. Simmer 3 minutes and gradually add 1 cup of stock from the pot while stirring. Remove from the heat.

Add the sour cream to the thickened mixture, stirring well, and return to the large pot. Heat through over low heat. Return the beef cubes to the sauce for a few minutes and serve.
Serves 25

Nutritional Meat Loaf

10 pounds freshly ground lean beef
    (or combination beef, veal, and pork; have
    butcher grind together)
1½ teaspoons cinnamon
1¼ cups ground onions
2 tablespoons thyme
3 tablespoons sea salt
3 tablespoons nutritional yeast

3 tablespoons soy lecithin powder
2½ cups rolled oats
5 eggs, beaten
6 cups yogurt
Tomato sauce or ketchup

Preheat oven to 325°.

Except for the tomato sauce or ketchup, mix ingredients together in order given, sprinkling cinnamon over a little at a time and mixing well. Mixture should be moist but hold together fairly well. More oats or yogurt may be added if needed.

Divide mixture into 6 well-oiled 5″ x 9″ loaf pans, about 2¾ pounds per pan.

Score tops of loaves in diagonal lines with tip of spatula and fill indentations with tomato sauce or ketchup.

Bake at 325° for 1 hour, or 1½ hours if made partly with pork.

Serve with tomato sauce, ketchup, or yogurt.
Serves 50

High Nutrition Meat Loaf

1½ pounds freshly ground lean beef
½ pound freshly ground calf or beef liver
    (Have butcher grind these together.)
1 onion, chopped fine
½ cup rolled oats
1 teaspoon sea salt
1 egg
¾ cup tomato juice
Tomato sauce or ketchup

Preheat oven to 325°.

Combine all ingredients (except tomato sauce or ketchup) and form into a loaf. Place in an oiled pan and bake at 325° for 1 hour.

The loaf may be scored before baking by pressing the flat side of a knife in diagonal stripes along the top. Fill the indentations with tomato sauce or ketchup.
Serves 6

Roast Beef Mold With Horseradish Sauce

2 envelopes unflavored gelatin
3 cups beef stock (see page 156)
¼ teaspoon sea salt
¼ cup Greek salad dressing (see recipe below)
1 pound carrots, cooked and cut in strips
1 cup sliced beets (canned or fresh cooked)
1 pound asparagus tips, cooked
1 pound cooked roast beef or pot roast, sliced thin

In a saucepan, sprinkle gelatin over 1 cup of beef stock to soften.

Place over low heat and stir until gelatin is dissolved. Remove from heat, stir in remaining stock and salt.

Pour ½ cup stock mixture into 2-quart casserole. Set in a pan of ice and water to speed setting. Refrigerate remaining stock mixture.

Make *Greek Salad Dressing:*

½ cup wine vinegar
2 garlic cloves, crushed
1 teaspoon sea salt
¼ teaspoon pepper
½ teaspoon oregano
1 cup olive oil

Combine seasonings with vinegar in a bottle and shake well. Add oil and shake again.

In separate small bowls, marinate the carrots and beets in the Greek salad dressing.

Arrange asparagus wheel-fashion on gelatin in casserole.

Cut beef into 2"x3" strips. Place half of the strips over the asparagus, making two layers.

Remove carrots from dressing with a slotted spoon and layer over meat.

Make two more layers with remaining meat.

Lift beets from Greek salad dressing and place on top.

Pour remaining stock mixture carefully over all and refrigerate for two hours or more.

To unmold, run knife or spatula around edge of casserole. Insert two straws on either side to break vacuum. Remove straws and invert on serving platter, shaking gently to release.

Serve with *Horseradish Sauce:*

>1 cup mayonnaise
>1 cup whipping cream
>1 tablespoon well-drained horseradish

>Mix well together.

Serves 4–6

Note: Dressing may be saved and used again.

Beef and Yogurt Loaf

>3 pounds freshly ground lean beef
>1/2 cup yogurt
>1/2 teaspoon cinnamon
>1 medium onion, chopped
>1 tablespoon thyme
>1 teaspoon sea salt
>1 tablespoon nutritional yeast
>1 tablespoon soy lecithin powder
>4 hard-boiled eggs
>Tomato sauce or ketchup

Preheat oven to 325°.

Mix ingredients together in order given (except tomato sauce or ketchup), sprinkling the cinnamon over a little at a time and mixing through well. Powdered cinnamon is more difficult to distribute evenly if added in one spot.

Take half of the meat and form the bottom half of the loaf. Place the hard-boiled eggs in a row, end to end, in the center; with the remaining meat mixture, form the top part of the loaf over and around the row of eggs. In the center of each slice there will be a slice of hard-boiled egg.

Score the top by pressing the flat side of a knife in diagonal stripes. Fill the indentations with tomato sauce or ketchup.

Bake at 325° for 1 hour.

Serves 8

Lamb Ring

2 pounds ground uncooked lamb
1 cup milk or meat stock
1 egg, slightly beaten
1 cup fine whole-wheat cracker crumbs
2 tablespoons minced onion
1 green pepper, chopped fine
2 tablespoons chopped parsley
1½ teaspoons sea salt
⅛ teaspoon pepper
1½ pounds (2 cups) cooked lima beans
1½ pounds (3 cups) cooked corn kernels

Preheat oven to 350°.

Combine ingredients, except corn and lima beans, and mix thoroughly.

Turn into oiled ring mold and bake at 350° for one hour

Unmold on hot serving plate; fill center with corn and surround lamb ring with lima beans.
Serves 6

Ragout of Lamb

16 pounds lamb, cut into 1½-inch cubes
3 medium onions, chopped
¼ cup chopped parsley
1 pound carrots, cut in strips
1 pound celery, cut in strips
1 cup cider vinegar
1 teaspoon peppercorns
½ teaspoon basil
2 teaspoons sea salt
6 cups water
8 pounds potatoes, peeled and cubed
¼ cup toasted wheat germ

Combine all ingredients in a heavy pot, except potatoes and wheat germ, and simmer gently about 1 hour or until meat is tender.

Add potatoes and cook 10 to 15 minutes or until tender but not mushy.

Put in warm serving dish and sprinkle with toasted wheat germ.

Serves 25

Baked Lamb With Eggplant

3 eggplant
Olive oil
¾ cup chopped onion
1 pound lean ground lamb
½ teaspoon sea salt
¼ teaspoon pepper
¼ teaspoon cinnamon
¼ teaspoon nutmeg
½ cup raw, natural pignolias (pine nuts)
    or slivered almonds
Butter
Olive oil
12 ounces tomato puree
¾ cup water

Preheat oven to 400°.

Peel eggplant and cut into eighths lengthwise. Line up the pieces closely in an oiled baking dish. Drizzle with a little olive oil and bake at 400° for 10 minutes. Remove and allow to cool. Turn oven down to 350°.

In the meantime, make the following lamb filling:

Sauté onions in a little oil until soft. Add the ground lamb and cook through briefly, stirring often.

Drain off the fat and place the meat in a bowl. Stir in the spices, salt, and pepper. Brown the nuts in a little butter and add them to the meat mixture.

Fill the spaces between the eggplant pieces (which form a V) with the lamb filling. Combine the tomato puree with ¾ cup water and pour over the eggplant and meat.

Bake at 350° for 20 minutes.

Serves 6

Kibbee With Cracked Wheat

1½ cups fine cracked wheat
2 pounds lean ground lamb
1 onion, chopped fine
¼ cup pignolias (pine nuts)
¼ teaspoon cinnamon
½ teaspoon sea salt
½ cup cold water
Yogurt

Preheat oven to 350°.

Rinse the cracked wheat in some water and squeeze dry in the palm of the hand.

Combine cracked wheat, lamb, chopped onion, nuts, cinnamon, and salt. Knead well with hands. Add ½ cup cold water and form into 3½" to 4" loaves.

Traditionally, kibbee is served raw in the Near East. Sometimes they just spoon a little melted butter or yogurt over it. It is a national dish in Lebanon and Syria. In fact, a Sunday dinner is not considered complete without a serving of kibbee.

Most Americans prefer cooked kibbee, which is indeed delicious. Place the small loaves in a baking pan and bake at 350° for 15 to 20 minutes, depending upon the size.

Serve with yogurt on the side.

Serves 6

Stuffed Green Peppers

6 large green peppers
½ cup pignolias (pine nuts) or slivered almonds
Oil or butter
1 onion, chopped
2 pounds ground lamb
½ teaspoon sea salt
¼ teaspoon pepper
1 teaspoon cinnamon
¼ cup chopped parsley
3 tomatoes
Dried mint (or chopped fresh)

Preheat oven 400°.

Split peppers, remove stems and seeds. Parboil 5 minutes and drain.

Brown nuts in oil or butter and put into a large bowl.

Sauté onions until soft, add lamb and cook through, stirring. Add to the nuts along with salt, pepper, cinnamon, and parsley.

Scald tomatoes, peel, and slice each into 4 slices.

Fill the pepper halves with the lamb mixture, place a slice of tomato on top of each, and sprinkle with mint.

Place peppers next to each other in a baking dish. Put a little boiling water in the bottom, up to ¼" of the pepper, and bake at 400° for 20 minutes.

Serves 6

Lamb Shanks

>   6 lamb shanks, about 1 pound each
>   Whole-wheat flour
>   Safflower oil
>   6 garlic cloves
>   1 cup red wine or sherry
>   1 teaspoon thyme
>   1 teaspoon sea salt

Wipe off lamb shanks with a damp cloth and dredge with flour.

Brown well in oil and remove from heat.

Peel the garlic cloves and insert between the meat and the bone at the large end. Push in as far as possible.

Put the shanks in a heavy pot with the wine, thyme, and salt. Add just enough water to barely cover the shanks. Simmer for 1 to 1½ hours or until tender.

Serves 6

Note: For a complete meal, 4 cups of vegetables may be added before last 5 minutes of cooking. The vegetables may be chopped onions, carrots, turnips, celery, or tomatoes, and green vegetables, such as cut green beans or peas may be added. If lima beans or potatoes are added, allow more time for cooking.

Pilaf of Chicken Livers

Rice Pilaf
Tomato Sauce
Chicken Livers
Bunches of fresh parsley

Rice Pilaf

2 tablespoons butter
2 tablespoons chopped onions
1½ cups brown rice
3 cups boiling chicken stock

Sauté onions in butter in heavy pot until transparent. Add rice and boiling stock and cook until rice is tender but still a little moist, 30 to 35 minutes. Add more water or stock if needed.

Tomato Sauce

3 pounds fresh tomatoes
5 tablespoons olive oil
1½ teaspoons sea salt
¼ teaspoon pepper
1 garlic clove
1 tablespoon parsley, chopped

Wash tomatoes and cut in half. Put them in a heavy pan with oil, salt, pepper, garlic, and parsley. Cover and simmer over low heat for 30 minutes.

Strain through a fine sieve.

Chicken Livers

3 tablespoons unrefined olive oil
1 pound chicken livers
½ teaspoon sea salt
¼ teaspoon pepper

Sauté chicken livers quickly in oil with salt and pepper.

To assemble dish, make a ring of the rice pilaf and put the chicken livers in the center. Pour the tomato sauce over the livers. Garnish dish with bunches of parsley.

Serves 6

Parsley

Curried Chicken Livers on Toast

2 pounds chicken livers
1 tablespoon curry powder
1 garlic clove, crushed
1 tablespoon powdered ginger
1 tablespoon mustard powder
1 tablespoon sea salt
Unrefined olive oil
¼ cup dry sherry
8 thin slices whole-grain toast
Fresh parsley for garnish

Wash livers and cut in half.

Combine the curry powder, garlic, ginger, mustard, and salt.

Heat 2 tablespoons olive oil in a skillet and cook the spices for one minute, stirring. This releases their fragrance.

Add 2 more tablespoons olive oil and sauté the chicken livers until nicely browned on all sides.

Add the sherry and simmer, scraping up all the good particles from the pan. Cover and set aside.

Toast the bread on both sides under the broiler, cut in half diagonally, and arrange on a warm platter. Warm the chicken livers for a moment, adding more sherry if needed, and spoon onto the toast points. Garnish with fresh parsley.

Serves 8

Liver München

1 pound beef liver
Unrefined olive oil and butter
4 bananas, sliced
1 large onion, sliced
¼ teaspoon sea salt
½ teaspoon thyme
½ teaspoon rosemary
½ teaspoon nutmeg
4 tablespoons sherry

Sauté liver and onions in a mixture of oil and butter with the spices. Add the bananas and brown them.

Place the liver, onions, and bananas on a warm platter, leaving the juices in the pan.

Add sherry to the juices over low heat and stir until the pan is clean. Pour this over the liver, onions, and bananas. Serve at once.
Serves 4

Beef Liver Casserole

4 pounds beef liver, scraped
1 cup chopped onions
2 tablespoons chopped parsley
Oil
1 tablespoon brewer's yeast
½ teaspoon pepper
1 teaspoon sea salt
4 loaves rye bread or Italian bread, sliced thin
2 cups sour cream
6 eggs, beaten

Preheat oven to 400°.

Remove the membrane from the liver and put liver in a bowl.

Cover with boiling water and set aside for 10 minutes.

Sauté onions with parsley lightly in oil and set aside.

Scrape the liver and combine with yeast, pepper, and salt. Add it to the onions and parsley and simmer over low heat for 5 minutes.

In a buttered casserole place alternate layers of bread and liver mixture.

Combine the sour cream with the eggs and pour over casserole. Bake at 400° for 30 minutes.
Serves 25

Kidneys in Mustard Sauce

8 to 12 lamb kidneys or 3 to 4 veal kidneys
4 tablespoons butter
1 tablespoon minced shallots or scallions
¼ cup lemon juice
¼ cup sherry
1½ tablespoons Dijon-type mustard
3 tablespoons butter
Sea salt and pepper
1 tablespoon nutritional yeast

Remove membranes and hard parts of kidneys and wash in cold water.

Melt 4 tablespoons butter and add the kidneys. Simmer gently, uncovered, stirring occasionally. Lamb kidneys take about 5 minutes to cook; veal kidneys take about 10 minutes. They should be pink inside when sliced. Remove kidneys to a warm plate.

Add the shallots or onions to the pan and cook for a moment. Add the lemon juice and sherry and boil until the liquid has reduced to 4 tablespoons.

Blend mustard with 3 tablespoons butter and stir into the liquid in the pan. Add a dash of salt and pepper and stir in the yeast.

Cut the kidneys crosswise into slices ⅛'' thick and return them with their juices to the pan.

When ready to serve, heat them through for a moment without boiling.
Serves 4

Kidney Creole

2 veal kidneys
2 tablespoons brown rice flour
2 tablespoons whole-wheat flour
Unrefined olive oil
2 tablespoons minced shallots or green onions
1 green pepper, chopped
1 stalk celery, chopped
1 clove garlic, crushed
1 cup tomato sauce
½ teaspoon thyme
1 bay leaf, crushed
½ teaspoon sea salt
1 tablespoon nutritional yeast
¼ teaspoon freshly ground pepper

Remove membranes and hard parts of kidneys, split and wash in cold water.

Combine flours. Dredge kidneys in flour and sauté in oil about 5 minutes and remove from pan.

Put the shallots, green pepper, celery, and garlic in pan, adding a little more oil if needed. Sauté about 3 minutes and add tomato sauce with thyme, bay leaf, salt, yeast, and pepper. Simmer 5 minutes.

Return kidneys to pan. Mix well with the sauce. Simmer gently 10 minutes.
Serves 6

Ginger–Sesame Chicken

Frying chicken, cut up
Lemon juice
Powdered ginger
Rosemary
Sesame seeds

Preheat oven to 325°.

Wash chicken, pat dry, and place in baking dish, skin side up.

Sprinkle with lemon juice. Spread each piece of chicken with powdered ginger and sprinkle with rosemary.

Bake at 325° for 45 minutes, spooning liquid over chicken pieces two or three times during baking.

Broil a few minutes until nicely browned. Sprinkle each piece well with sesame seeds and broil a few seconds longer or until seeds are browned.

Serves 3–4

Green Peppers

Chicken Paprika

3 tablespoons butter
3 tablespoons sesame seed oil
3 medium onions, chopped
3 tablespoons paprika
5 pounds frying chicken, cut up
2 cups chicken broth
1 teaspoon sea salt
2 tablespoons dry sherry
2 tablespoons arrowroot
2 cups yogurt

Melt butter with oil in a large, heavy pot. Add the onions and paprika, cooking until golden.

Add chicken pieces, chicken broth, salt, and sherry. Simmer 1 hour.

Add arrowroot to yogurt and stir into pot slowly over very low heat. Heat through; do not boil.

Serve with whole wheat or artichoke noodles.

Serves 6

Creamed Sweetbreads

1½ pounds sweetbreads
6 mushrooms, cleaned and sliced
Butter
⅓ cup cream
1 tablespoon lemon juice
Sea salt and freshly ground pepper

Saúte mushrooms for a minute or two in a little butter. Remove from the pan.

Wash sweetbreads and remove membranes.

Add a little more butter to the pan and sauté the sweetbreads over very low heat without letting them brown. Remove them to a warm platter and place the sliced mushrooms over them.

Add the cream and lemon juice to the pan, stirring. Season to taste with salt and pepper. Pour over sweetbreads and serve.
Serves 6

Note: Sweetbreads are delicate and perishable. They should be used very fresh. Otherwise, cook the sweetbreads in boiling water with 1 teaspoon salt and 1 tablespoon lemon juice. Cook for 15 minutes, drain, remove loose membrane, and refrigerate for a short time only.

Baked Chicken With Apples

25 pounds frying chicken, cut up
2 tablespoons sea salt
¾ cup butter
¾ cup safflower oil
6 pounds cooking apples, peeled and sliced
¼ cup raw unfiltered honey
1 cup apple cider

Preheat oven to 375°.

Sprinkle chicken with salt and sauté lightly in butter combined with oil.

Place in a buttered baking pan with sliced apples. Drizzle honey over chicken; add cider and cover the dish.

Bake at 375° for 40 minutes or until chicken is tender.
Serves 25

Chicken Marengo With Brown Rice

3 to 4 pounds chicken breasts and legs
Whole-wheat flour
Safflower or sesame oil
1 cup water or chicken stock
12 small white onions, peeled
4 tomatoes, peeled and seeded and cut into quarters
½ green pepper, sliced
½ cup pitted black olives
¼ teaspoon Italian seasoning or allspice
¼ pound mushrooms, sliced
Butter
½ cup dry white wine
1 cup brown rice
2½ cups water
¼ teaspoon sea salt

Dredge chicken pieces with flour and brown in oil.

Transfer chicken to a heavy pot and add 1 cup water or stock, onions, tomatoes, green pepper, olives, and seasonings. Simmer until tender, about 40 minutes.

In a skillet, sauté mushrooms in a little butter and add to the pot with the wine. Simmer 5 minutes.

In another saucepan combine the rice with 2½ cups water and salt. Bring to a boil, cover, and simmer gently until water is absorbed, about 35 minutes. Drain and keep warm by returning to saucepan.

Add a little salt to the chicken dish if needed and serve with rice.
Serves 6

Lemons

Chicken Tetrazzini

2 frying chickens, cut up
3 tablespoons safflower oil
½ pound mushrooms, caps and stems, sliced thin
½ pound artichoke or spinach spaghetti
3 tablespoons butter
2 tablespoons brown rice or oat flour
2 cups chicken broth
1 cup cream
3 tablespoons sherry
1 teaspoon sea salt
¼ teaspoon pepper
½ teaspoon nutmeg
½ cup grated Parmesan cheese

Cover the chicken with boiling water and simmer until tender, about 40 minutes. Remove the chicken pieces and, when cool enough to handle, cut the meat into strips and set aside.

Return the bones and skin to the pot and cook the chicken stock down until 2 cups remain. Strain the broth and place in freezer so that the fat will surface.

Heat oil in a skillet and saute the mushroom caps and stems. Set aside.

Cook the spaghetti in boiling water according to instructions on the package. Drain and keep warm.

Remove the chicken broth from freezer, skim off fat, and bring broth to a boil in the saucepan.

In a saucepan, melt 3 tablespoons butter, add the flour, simmer for 3 minutes, stirring.

Gradually pour in the warm chicken broth, stirring until smooth and thickened. Add the cream, sherry, salt, pepper, and nutmeg.

Combine the cooked mushrooms and spaghetti and pour half of the sauce over it. Then turn it into a buttered baking dish.

Add the other half of the sauce to the chicken strips.

Make a hole in the center of the spaghetti mixture and pour the chicken mixture into the hole.

Sprinkle with Parmesan cheese and brown lightly under broiler.

Serves 6

Rock Cornish Hens in a Pot

4 1-pound Rock Cornish hens
Safflower oil
1 tablespoon whole-wheat flour
1 teaspoon salt
¼ teaspoon pepper
1 teaspoon thyme
2 tablespoons Worcestershire sauce
1 cup red wine
2 tablespoons lemon juice
8 small white onions
8 mushrooms
Butter
Fresh parsley or fresh dill

In a heavy pot sauté Cornish hens in oil. When golden on all sides, remove from pot and stir in flour, salt, pepper, thyme, Worcestershire sauce, wine, and lemon juice.

Return hens to pot, cover, and simmer 45 minutes.

In a separate skillet, sauté onions in a little butter and add to pot with hens. Then sauté mushrooms and add to pot. Simmer 5 to 10 minutes.

Serve garnished with sprigs of parsley or fresh dill.

Serves 4

Marinated Chicken

2 frying chickens, cut up, or 6 chicken breasts
1 cup sesame seed oil
½ cup Chablis or chicken broth, or combination
¼ cup tamari sauce
2 tablespoons raw sesame seeds

Wipe off chicken with a damp cloth and place in a dish.

Combine the oil, Chablis or chicken broth, tamari, and sesame seeds. Pour over the chicken. Set aside to marinate for 1 hour, moving chicken pieces around some to marinate well.

Lift the chicken pieces out of the marinade and place in a baking pan. Bake at 350° for about 45 minutes or until done, brushing with the marinade several times during cooking period.

Broil a moment to brown further if needed.
Serves 6–8

Breast of Chicken Tarragon

4 breasts of chicken, split
1 small onion, sliced thin
1 small carrot, sliced thin
¾ teaspoon dried tarragon or 3 fresh sprigs
3 tablespoons butter
3 tablespoons brown rice flour
Sea salt and pepper
Dried tarragon or fresh tarragon leaves

Remove skin and any fat from chicken breasts and place in a pot with the onion, carrot, and tarragon. Add water to cover and simmer until tender, about 25 minutes.

Remove chicken breasts to a warm platter and keep warm.

Boil chicken stock down until it is reduced to 2 cups.

In a separate saucepan, melt butter, add flour, and simmer 3 minutes. Add the 2 cups of stock and season to taste with salt and pepper. Simmer 5 more minutes, stirring frequently.

Pour sauce over chicken and garnish with a little dried tarragon or with fresh tarragon leaves.
Serves 6

Baked Filet of Sole

12 pounds filet of sole or flounder
2 teaspoons sea salt
Brown rice flour
Butter
6 tablespoons butter
6 tablespoons brown rice flour
3 pints milk, warmed
3 eggs, beaten
3 egg yolks, beaten
1/2 teaspoon sea salt
1/8 teaspoon pepper
1 teaspoon kelp powder or granules
1 teaspoon nutmeg
1 tablespoon lemon juice
1 teaspoon Worcestershire sauce
3/4 cup grated Parmesan cheese
3/4 cup raw wheat germ

Sprinkle fish with 2 teaspoons salt and dip lightly in brown rice flour. Place in buttered baking pan and dot with butter.

Broil for 10 minutes.

Melt the 6 tablespoons butter, add 6 tablespoons brown rice flour, and simmer, stirring, for 3 minutes. Stir in warmed milk and simmer 2 more minutes.

Combine eggs, egg yolks, salt, pepper, kelp, nutmeg, lemon juice, and Worcestershire sauce. Pour over fish.

Combine Parmesan cheese and wheat germ and sprinkle on top.

Bake at 350° for 10 minutes.
Serves 25

Baked Swordfish Steak

3 pounds swordfish steak 1½'' thick
¼ cup melted butter
Sea salt
Paprika
Pepper
Kelp powder or granules
1 cup stuffed olives, chopped

Preheat oven to 350°.

Wash swordfish and place in buttered baking dish; pour melted butter over it.

Sprinkle with salt, paprika, pepper, and kelp. Then distribute the chopped olives over the swordfish.

Bake at 350° for 50 minutes.
Serves 8

Turbot Au Gratin

2 cups Mornay Sauce (recipe below)
1 cup sliced mushrooms
Butter or Safflower oil
1½ cups flaked cooked turbot
Sea salt
Pepper
¼ cup grated Cheddar cheese
½ cup raw wheat germ
Butter

Preheat oven 350°.

Mornay Sauce

4 tablespoons butter
4 tablespoons brown rice flour
2 cups milk, warmed
½ cup grated Cheddar cheese

Melt butter in saucepan, add flour, and simmer 3 minutes.

Add warmed milk gradually, stirring, and simmer 2 more minutes. Add ½ cup grated cheese and stir until blended.

Sauté sliced mushrooms in a little butter and add to the Mornay sauce. Stir in the flaked fish and season to taste.

Turn into a baking dish and sprinkle with ¼ cup grated cheese and the wheat germ. Dot with butter and bake at 350° until brown, about 10 minutes.

Serves 6

Broiled Salmon Hollandaise

Hollandaise (blender method)

> 4 egg yolks
> ¼ pound butter (1 stick)
> 1 tablespoon lemon juice
> 2 tablespoons water

Place the egg yolks in blender.

Melt the butter with the lemon juice and water.

Blend egg yolks a second, then add a little melted butter and blend a second more. Add the rest of the butter in a stream; the thickish residue of butter in the pan may be left out, using only the clarified butter.

Set aside until ready to use.

> 3 pounds fresh salmon
> ¼ cup lemon juice
> Butter

Wipe salmon off with a damp cloth and place on a buttered broiling pan.

Pour lemon juice over salmon and dot with butter. Broil for 12 minutes.

Remove pan with salmon onto a heat-proof surface and cover the fish with hollandaise sauce.

Return to broiler and broil until lightly browned and bubbly. Serve at once.

Serves 6

Scalloped Tuna or Crab Meat With Noodles

1½ pounds whole-wheat, spinach, or artichoke noodles
3 gallons boiling water
3 tablespoons sea salt (optional)
1½ pounds butter or 3⅓ cups oil
1⅓ cups whole-wheat flour
1 gallon milk, warmed
4 egg yolks
½ cup ground onion
2 tablespoons sea salt
3 cups almond slivers
4 pounds tuna or canned crab meat
2½ cups grated Parmesan cheese

Cook noodles in boiling water to which 3 tablespoons salt have been added if desired. Cook for 10 to 15 minutes, or until tender, and drain.

Preheat oven to 350°.

Melt butter, add flour, and simmer 3 minutes. Add warm milk and simmer, stirring, for 3 minutes. Remove from heat.

Pour a little of the sauce into another pan, then add the egg yolks, blending well. Return pan with sauce back to low heat and slowly add egg mixture, stirring well. Add onion, salt, almonds, and fish.

Spoon the fish mixture into individual casseroles or shallow baking pans and sprinkle with grated Parmesan.

Bake at 350° for 45 minutes.
Serves 50–60

Baked Turbot Filets

Turbot filets
Sesame seed oil
Lemon juice
Paprika
Soybeans, roasted
Parsley or watercress

Heat oven to 350°.

Line as many turbot filets as desired in a shallow, oiled baking pan.

Sprinkle with lemon juice (about ¼ cup to 6 filets), dot with oil, and sprinkle generously with paprika.

Bake for 15 minutes. Broil 5 minutes or less, until browned.

Remove from broiler, sprinkle with soybeans, and return to broiler until the soybeans have browned.

Garnish with clumps of parsley or watercress.

Acorn Squash Stuffed With Tuna

4 medium acorn squash
Sesame oil
2 7-ounce cans tuna packed in spring water, drained
½ medium onion, minced
½ cup celery, minced
1 teaspoon sea salt
½ teaspoon pepper
½ teaspoon kelp powder or granules
½ teaspoon thyme
½ cup whole-wheat bread crumbs
½ cup raw wheat germ
2 tablespoons melted butter

Preheat oven to 400°.

Wash squash, cut into halves, and remove seeds. Spread oil over surface of inside of squash and turn cut side down in a shallow baking dish. Bake about 35 minutes until tender.

Remove squash from oven, scoop out, and reserve shells.

Mash the squash and mix with tuna, onion, celery, salt, pepper, kelp, and thyme. Spoon lightly into squash shells.

Combine bread crumbs and wheat germ and sprinkle on top. Sprinkle with melted butter and return to oven for 10 minutes.
Serves 8

Stuffed Crabs

25 large crabs
¼ cup cider vinegar
1 tablespoon sea salt
1 tablespoon onion, chopped fine
¾ cup butter or safflower oil
1 tablespoon parsley, chopped
2 teaspoons thyme
3 pounds sole, cooked and shredded
2 teaspoons sea salt
½ teaspoon pepper
1 cup lemon juice
1 tablespoon Worcestershire sauce
¼ cup bran flakes
½ cup grated Parmesan cheese
Butter

Scrub crabs thoroughly with a brush in cold water. Tie each one and drop into boiling water to which the vinegar and 1 tablespoon salt have been added. Simmer for 15 minutes.

Crack the claws and legs and remove the meat. Break off the pieces which fold under the body from the rear and open shells by forcing a strong knife into the opening. Remove the sand bags, gills, the spongy parts, and cut the good parts into pieces. Combine them with the meat from the claws and legs.

Preheat oven to 400°.

Sauté onions until transparent in the butter; add parsley, thyme, and shredded sole, mixing it all through. Add salt, pepper, lemon juice, and Worcestershire sauce, and bring to a boil.

Stuff the crab shells with this mixture. Place the shells in a pan.

Mix the bran flakes and grated Parmesan and sprinkle over the stuffed crab shells. Dot with butter and bake at 400° for 15 to 20 minutes.

Serves 25

Peanuts

Lemon

Honey

Eggs

Breads, Rolls, Muffins, Biscuits

Rye Flour

Dates

Nutmeg

Bread

Inasmuch as breads, rolls, muffins, and biscuits are staple foods eaten regularly and often, we realize how much good nutrition we have missed by eating these staple foods made of refined flours, which are sadly depleted, and to which sugar and a large assortment of chemicals have been added. So-called "enriched" flour does not contain some of the vitamins and is stripped of the major portions of at least a dozen minerals and trace minerals, which are essential to mental and physical health. Two minerals are returned to "enriched" flour: calcium and iron. The form of iron used, however, is poorly assimilated by the body.

We realize at the same time how many vital food elements we may now introduce into our homes by learning how to use whole-grain flours, powders, and meals in our baking.

Baking with natural ingredients opens up an entirely new world in taste treats. Whole-grain flours, seeds, meals, and powders may be used in an endless variety of combinations. I would urge every cook to experiment with these ingredients, exchanging natural flours, oils, and sweeteners for others in the recipes given here.

Whole-Grain Flours and Meals

Stone-ground flours and meals are most desirable nutritionally because the slow-moving stones used in the grinding process generate considerably less heat than the high-speed roller mills used in the processing of white flour. The high-speed rollers strip grain of its germ and a high percentage of its valuable nutrients. Whole-grain flours and meals include:

Whole-wheat flour	Potato flour
Whole-wheat pastry flour	Millet flour
Graham flour (wheat with	Corn flour
a part of the bran removed)	Gluten flour
Buckwheat flour	Barley flour
Rye flour	Bean flours
Triticale flour (made from	Peanut flour
a cross of wheat and	Soy flour
rye grains)	Corn meal

Wheat germ flour	Oatmeal
Brown rice flour	Sunflower seed meal
Oat flour	Sesame seed meal

In recipes calling for sifted flours, return the particles left in the sifter to the flour.

Always sift soy flour; it tends to be lumpy. Soy flour browns quickly. When using it, lower the oven temperature by 25 degrees.

Refrigerate whole-grain flours. If purchased in quantity, they may be frozen and the container in the refrigerator refilled when needed.

Whole-grain flours come in small quantities so it is possible to keep a good variety on hand. I keep mine lined up in a pan on the bottom shelf of my refrigerator for easy access.

Sometimes white flour is used in combination with whole-grain flours to produce a special texture. If white flour is called for, use unbleached flour and fortify it with nonfat dry milk, soy flour, and wheat germ. I recommend using the Cornell Formula, which was developed by Dr. Clive M. McCay and his associates at Cornell University.

Cornell Formula

1 tablespoon soy flour
1 tablespoon nonfat dry milk
1 teaspoon wheat germ

Put soy flour, dry milk, and wheat germ in a measuring cup and fill the cup with unbleached flour to reach the 1-cup level. Blend the mixture well.

Note: I recommend noninstant nonfat dry milk powder because it has undergone less processing and is, therefore, more nutritious.

Liquids

In baking with whole grains, the overall proportion of liquids to dry ingredients varies considerably due to the ability of the grains to absorb moisture. It is difficult, therefore, to specify exact amounts of either, particularly in yeast mixtures. Recipes give approximate amounts. More flour or liquid may have to be added according to consistency desired; that consistency is usually described as a guide.

Adapting Recipes Made With Refined Ingredients

Per each cup of refined, "enriched" flour use

¾ cup whole-grain flours

or

1½ cups oatmeal

or

1 cup corn flour

or

1 cup Cornell Formula flour

Substitute sugar with half as much honey, unsulphured molasses, or pure maple syrup. Replace corn syrup with the same amount of honey, unsulphured molasses, or pure maple syrup.

If herbs or spices are added, add ¼ teaspoon per cup of flour.

If margarine or shortening are called for, use butter or oil in same quantity. Or use butter combined with safflower oil (½ cup oil blended into 1 pound pure creamery butter, stored in container in refrigerator).

Use ⅓ less oil.

Fortifying Agents

To add further nutrition to baked goods, any of the following may be used satisfactorily:

Wheat germ	Milk
Rice polishings	Eggs
Nonfat dry milk	Nutritional yeast
Soy flour	Bone meal

If eggs are added to a recipe, reduce the liquid in the recipe by one-fifth and the baking powder by ½ teaspoon per egg.

Exchanging Whole-Grain Flours in Bread

In exchanging whole-grain flours in baking, it is important to bear in mind that wheat and rye flours are the only flours which contain an appreciable amount of gluten. Hard wheat (winter wheat) flour contains the most. Gluten gives yeast dough its elasticity and is developed in kneading; gluten also gives bread its form. Therefore, in exchanging flours for variety, be sure to include some wheat or rye flours or add some gluten flour to compensate. Gluten flour is wheat flour with the starch removed. For each cup of low-gluten flour (such as soy, corn, oat, or barley) use ½ cup gluten flour and count it in the overall measurement of flour for your bread recipe.

Leavening Agents

Leavening agents are yeast, eggs, baking powder, and baking soda. From the nutritional standpoint, yeast and eggs are most desirable and to be used where possible because of the added nutrition they impart to baked goods. My recipes call for baking powder rather than baking soda because baking powder has half the sodium content. However, when baking powder is called for, use the low-sodium, aluminum-free variety. You will find these supplies in natural food stores.

Yeast Breads and Rolls

Bread-making is an art, but fortunately it is one that is easily mastered; it is also very rewarding. There are a few rules to follow, but there is also much room for creativity because of the number of ingredients and methods that may be successfully used and interchanged. A few rules are necessary because with yeast we are handling living organisms which must be kept alive, active, and controlled. Freshness, temperature, humidity, and altitude all influence the rising of bread. We also are dealing with a variety of whole grains with their varying characteristics. The following rules are helpful to know:

1. All ingredients and utensils should be at room temperature. If flour has just been removed from the refrigerator, warm the measured amount needed in a pan in a warm oven until the chill is off. If your bowls are cold, put them in the oven too, or pour hot water in them.

2. Yeast should be refrigerated. It must be fresh. Recipes calling for dry yeast measure it by tablespoons. Some premeas-

ured, packaged dry yeast packets contain something less than a tablespoon and may also contain a chemcial preservative. Hence, I purchase mine in 8-ounce packages at a natural food store. This yeast comes in a foil container which may be folded after opening and placed in the refrigerator. If you bake often, it is more economical to purchase yeast in larger quantities. Keep it in an airtight container in the refrigerator or in a cool, dry place.

3. In reducing a bread recipe, cut all ingredients in half, including the yeast. When doubling a recipe, increase everything proportionately except the yeast. The amount of yeast remains the same because yeast action is more rapid in large quantities.

4. The liquid used in dissolving yeast should be warm. It should not be lukewarm (which is usually too cool by the way many people determine it), and it should not be hot. I judge the temperature with my little finger—if the water feels warm but has no bite, it seems just right. If yeast does not activate (bubble) within 5 to 10 minutes of being dissolved in water, start over. It means the water was either too cold or too hot, and the yeast will not work properly in your dough. Ginger, honey, molasses, and potato water (water in which a potato has been boiled) all encourage the action of yeast; when any are called for in the recipe, add them to the yeast and water mixture in the beginning. Potato water also helps keep bread moist and aids the yeast in the whole process of baking; the starch feeds the yeast slowly and consistently.

5. To knead bread, flatten it out into a large circle on a lightly floured board. Lift the far edge of the dough and fold it over toward you to the near edge. Press down firmly with the palms of the hands and swing the dough around, repeating the process and adding flour to the board as needed. Sometimes it is helpful to oil the hands slightly. Knead the dough until it starts resisting the hand and is smooth.

6. To form a loaf of bread, punch down the risen dough and take off however much is needed for a loaf—for example, half if the recipe makes two loaves. Press the dough into a large oval, lift the far side and bring it to within a third of the near

edge and press the edge down to seal it well. Do the same thing by lifting the side near you and taking it to the far side to seal. Then take the left side and bring it two-thirds over and press it to seal; then fold other end completely over and under a little, pressing to seal. Turn loaf over and shape loaf, smoothing all sides. Place in a well-buttered pan, cover, and let rise again.

7. For the rising process, place the dough in a warm (75°– 85°) spot away from drafts. Some people place their dough on top of the refrigerator (if it feels warm there) or in an oven or dishwasher to keep it out of a draft. I live in a warm and very dry climate and have an often air-conditioned kitchen, so I set my oven at "warm" only long enough to take off the chill. Then I place a pan of hot water on the bottom rack of the oven and my dough, covered, on the center rack. If you live at high altitudes, watch the rising period carefully—yeast dough rises more rapidly at high altitudes.

8. Whole grains absorb fats readily. Therefore, it is important to oil or butter the bread pans generously so that the bread will not stick. I prefer butter; it not only greases the pan better, but adds flavor.

9. Brushing the top of the loaf with a slightly beaten egg yolk just before baking makes a richer crust.

10. Bread should be baked on the center rack of the oven.

11. Bread is done when it pulls away from the sides of the pan and when an inserted toothpick comes out clean. To release bread from pans, run a spatula around the edges. If the sides are not crusty, return the bread to the oven, with heat off, to dry out for 10 minutes. Remove the bread from the pan and cool on a rack.

12. Keep bread in the refrigerator or freezer. If I want to pull bread out of the freezer a few slices at a time, I first slice the loaf and freeze the slices separated on a baking sheet; they freeze quickly. I then line them up in a plastic bag and mark the bag before I return it to the freezer. When sliced bread is frozen in a loaf, the slices freeze together and may not be lifted out separately.

13. If bread crumbles when slicing, which happens with some whole-grain breads, put the loaf in the freezer for a short period of time.

The New Start Basic Dough

(For bread, dinner rolls, biscuits, sweet rolls, English muffins, and sourdough bread)

I pass on to you a basic yeast dough worked out by my son. I present it not only because it is delicious and versatile, but because it is an excellent way to start educating your family, and perhaps your own palate, to more nutritious foods. Hence the name "The New Start."

Make this dough, break off a part of it, such as half of it for a loaf of bread or some rolls, and refrigerate the rest to use in succeeding days as desired. After a week it becomes sourdough and can be broken off as desired or kept as a sourdough starter. The dough should be kept in an oiled crock or nonmetallic bowl twice the size of the dough. When dough is placed in the refrigerator, it will rise until thoroughly chilled. When it does, just punch it down.

    1 potato, cut into quarters
    3½ cups water
    1½ teaspoons sea salt

Boil potato in salted water until soft. Drain potato, reserving potato water. When cool, peel potato.

    ½ cup warm water
    2 tablespoons yeast
    ¼ teaspoon ginger powder
    1 teaspoon honey

Stir until smooth in a warm bowl and place in a warm (75°–85°) spot for 5 to 10 minutes until it bubbles.

Force potato through a strainer. Put it into a 1-quart container and fill to 3 cups with potato water. (Or use smaller measuring cups, accomplishing the same proportions).

> 1⅓ cups whole-wheat flour
> 1⅓ cups whole-rye flour
> 1⅓ cups Cornell Formula (combine 1⅓ tablespoons nonfat dry milk, 1⅓ tablespoons soy flour, and 2 teaspoons wheat germ, and fill measure up to 1⅓ cups with unbleached flour)

Sift flours together and return any particles left in sifter to the bowl.

Make a well in the flour and pour yeast into it, stirring together with a wooden spoon.

Add potato water ⅓ at a time and stir well. Cover and put in a warm area.

Scald 1½ cups milk and allow to cool down to warm.

Beat each of the following ingredients into the flour-yeast mixture:

> Scalded milk
> 2 tablespoons melted butter mixed with 2 tablespoons oil
> 2 tablespoons honey (measure in same spoon used for oil as the honey will slide off easily because of the oil)

Then work in 6 cups flour: 2 cups whole-wheat, 2 cups whole-rye, and 2 cups Cornell Formula (putting in each cup measure 1 tablespoon nonfat dry milk, 1 tablespoon soy flour, and 1 teaspoon wheat germ, then filling cup with unbleached flour).

Flour hands and knead dough on lightly floured board until stickiness is gone and dough starts to resist the hand. It should be smooth and elastic. Keep board lightly floured as flour is used up.

Oil bowl and rub ball of dough around in it to coat dough. Cover with a damp cloth and place in a warm area to rise until double to triple in bulk, from one to two hours.

Punch down dough and knead well for a few minutes to get air bubbles out. Cut by halves or fourths depending on number of loaves to be baked.

For each loaf of bread, pat dough out flat and evenly, pushing out any remaining bubbles. Fold near side over two-thirds of the way, pressing along edge to seal. Then bring far side over to near side, pressing along edge to seal. Fold end in two-thirds and press to seal; then fold other end completely and tuck under. Turn dough over and shape loaf, smoothing all sides. Place in well-buttered bread pan, cover, and let rise until double in bulk.

Preheat oven to 375°.

Brush top of loaf with beaten egg yolk and bake at 375° for 10 minutes. Reduce heat to 350° and bake 35 minutes longer.
Yield: 4 loaves

Note: In high altitudes, start oven at 400° and reduce to 375°

To make dinner rolls, biscuits, sweet rolls, English muffins, and sourdough bread, follow directions below. If dough has been refrigerated, remove it from the refrigerator and cut off the part you want to use. Return the rest of the dough to the refrigerator. Allow the dough to be used to warm up; this takes 30 minutes or so. When it is warmed up, turn it onto a lightly floured board and knead vigorously for a few minutes; return to bowl, cover with a damp cloth, and allow to rise until double in bulk. Then proceed with any of the following:

Dinner Rolls

Pull off pieces of dough about an inch or so in diameter, depending on the size of the rolls you wish to make. Shape them into round or oblong pieces and place them on a buttered baking sheet. Cover and allow to rise until double in bulk, about 30 minutes. Bake at 375° for 20 minutes or until browned.

Cloverleaf Rolls

Pull off pieces of dough and form balls ½ inch in diameter. Butter each section of a muffin pan and place 3 balls in the bottom of each. Cover and let rise until double in bulk, about 30 minutes. Bake at 375° for about 20 minutes or until browned.

Eggs

Parker House Rolls

Roll dough out to ⅓-inch thickness. Cut into 2½-inch rounds, brush butter on one half of each round, fold buttered half over to within one-fourth of the other edge, and press edge lightly. Place on buttered baking sheet, cover, and let rise until double in bulk, about 30 minutes. Bake at 375° for about 20 minutes or until brown.

Braided Rolls

Pinch off pieces of dough about 2 inches in diameter and roll each one into a rope on a floured board. Work with the fingers, rolling from the center out so that the rope will be even. Take 2 or 3 strands and pinch them together at one end. Then braid them and pinch other end to seal. Either bake them like that or wind each one into a little circle to form a round twist roll. Place on a buttered baking sheet, cover, and let rise until double in bulk, about 30 minutes. Bake at 375° for 15 to 20 minutes or until browned.

Sweet Rolls

Roll out on a slightly floured board into a large oval ½ inch thick. Brush with melted butter mixed with honey. Sprinkle with chopped nuts, cinnamon, and raisins, if desired. Roll up like a jelly roll, cut into inch slices, place next to each other on a buttered baking sheet, cover, and let rise until double in bulk, about 30 minutes. Bake at 400° for 15 minutes.

Biscuits

To one-fourth of the dough recipe, rub in 4 tablespoons softened butter. Knead well. Roll or pat out on floured board to ¼- to ½-inch thickness, as desired, and cut with biscuit cutter. Place on buttered baking sheets (place apart if you want them crisp and close together if you want them softer) and bake at 400° for 10 to 12 minutes.

English Muffins

Sprinkle board with corn meal and roll out dough to ½-inch thickness. Cut with large, round biscuit cutter. Leave rounds on board, cover, and let rise until double in bulk, about 30 minutes. Cook on a moderately hot, ungreased griddle 5 to 7 minutes a side.

Whole-Wheat Bread and Rolls

2 tablespoons yeast
¼ teaspoon ginger powder
½ cup warm water or warm potato water
¼ cup honey
2 cups warm milk
½ cup safflower oil
2 eggs, beaten
2 teaspoons sea salt
4 cups whole-wheat flour
1 cup oat flour
1 cup soy flour
Sesame seeds or poppy seads (optional)

In a large bowl combine yeast, ginger, warm water, and honey. Stir until dissolved and allow to prove (bubble), 5 to 10 minutes.

Add milk, oil, eggs, salt, and whole-wheat flour, mixing well. Sift soy flour with oat flour and add to whole wheat mixture.

Turn out on a lightly floured board and let rest for a few minutes.

Knead for 8 to 10 minutes or until dough is smooth and elastic and starts resisting the hand.

Place dough in a well-oiled bowl and turn all around to coat dough. Cover with a damp cloth and allow to rise until double in bulk, 1 to 2 hours.

Push down and cut in two. Cover half and set aside while preparing the other half for baking.

To shape loaves, flatten dough evenly into a large oval, pushing out any bubbles. Fold near side over two-thirds of the way to other side and press edge to seal. Then bring far side over to near two-thirds of the way and press along edge to seal. Fold one end over two-thirds and press to seal, then fold other end over completely and tuck under. Turn loaf over and form either into a loaf or a ball, smoothing sides and stretching slightly to under side. Place loaf in a well-buttered bread pan or place ball on a well-buttered baking sheet.

Cover and let rise until double in bulk

Preheat oven to 350°.

Brush loaf with beaten egg yolk and sprinkle with sesame or poppy seeds if desired.

Bake at 350° for 40 minutes or until browned and an inserted toothpick comes out clean.

For rolls, see instructions on pages 136-137 (under preceding recipe).

Yield: 4 loaves

Quick Breads, Muffins, Biscuits, Coffeecakes

Quick breads bring a wonderful variety of new flavors and textures into your menus and provide snacks with little time or effort expended in their making. You will enjoy trying them and then using your own choice of flours and meals. Some whole-grain breads are lighter than others and some are very firm depending upon the structure of the flour or meal used and upon the use of eggs and baking powder.

Because we have become accustomed to the blown-up squashable, and almost tasteless refined products which fill miles of shelves in our nation, we have forgotten, if we ever knew, what character natural ingredients impart to baked goods. Many young people have never known the delights of the definite flavors and interesting structures of breads made from whole grains, and they have never known breads that are free from the many chemicals and sugar which are such a part of most commercial and home-baked goods.

The following recipes are only a few of the innumerable combinations of natural ingredients available to all cooks who want to add great nutrition, as well as great flavor, to their meals. Have a variety of natural flours, meals, oils, and sweeteners on hand, and change the recipes around to suit your own tastes.

Some recipes for quick breads call for whole-wheat pastry flour, but the regular whole-wheat flour may be used. Whole-wheat pastry flour is made from soft wheat, has less gluten, and is a little finer; whole-wheat flour is made from hard wheat, which has more gluten and is, therefore, used in yeast breads.

Date–Nut Bread

1½ cups dates, chopped
2 tablespoons butter
1 cup boiling water
1 egg, beaten
1 teaspoon pure vanilla extract
½ cup whole-wheat pastry flour
½ cup oat flour
¼ cup soy flour
2 teaspoons baking powder
½ teaspoon sea salt
½ cup raw wheat germ
½ cup chopped nuts

Preheat oven to 350°.

In a large bowl put dates and butter. Pour hot water over them and stir until butter is melted. Allow mixture to cool.

Add vanilla to egg and stir into date mixture.

Sift together flours, baking powder, and salt. Stir in wheat germ.

Stir dry ingredients into date mixture and add nuts.

Pour into a well-buttered or -oiled 5″x9″ bread pan and bake at 350° for 45 to 50 minutes or until an inserted toothpick comes out clean.

Remove from pan by running spatula around the edge and cool on a rack.
Yield: 1 loaf

Raisin–Bran Bread

> 1¾ cup milk
> 1 cup bran
> 2 cups whole-wheat flour
> ¼ cup soy flour
> ¼ cup nonfat dry milk
> 1 teaspoon sea salt
> 2 teaspoons baking powder
> ½ cup raw wheat germ
> 3 eggs, beaten
> ¼ cup unsulphured molasses
> 1 cup raisins
> 1 cup chopped nuts

Preheat oven to 350°.

Pour milk over bran and set aside.

Sift together flours, dry milk, salt, and baking powder. Stir in wheat germ.

Stir bran and milk mixture into the dry ingredients. Add eggs and molasses, stirring well.

Add raisins and nuts and pour into well-oiled or -buttered 5″x9″ bread pan.

Bake at 350° for 45 to 50 minutes or until an inserted toothpick comes out clean.

Remove from pan by running a spatula around the edge, and cool on a rack.
Yield: 1 loaf

Bananas

Banana–Nut Bread

1½ cups whole-wheat pastry flour
¼ cup soy flour
2 tablespoons nonfat dry milk
¼ teaspoon salt
2 tablespoons raw wheat germ
4 eggs, yolks and whites beaten separately
½ cup sesame oil
½ cup honey
1 teaspoon pure vanilla extract
¼ cup milk
2 large, or 3 small, ripe bananas, mashed well
1 cup chopped nuts

Preheat oven to 350°.

Sift flours, dry milk, and salt together. Stir in wheat germ.

Combine egg yolks, oil, honey, vanilla, milk, bananas, and nuts, and fold in beaten egg whites.

Pour into a well-buttered or -oiled 5"x9" bread pan and bake at 350° for 45 to 50 minutes or until an inserted toothpick comes out clean.

Remove from pan by running a spatula around edge and cool on a rack.
Yield: 1 loaf

No-Knead Bread

2 tablespoons dry yeast
¼ teaspoon ginger powder
3 cups warm water
¼ cup unsulphured molasses
3 cups whole-wheat flour
3 cups triticale or graham flour
¾ cup soy flour
¾ cup barley flour
3 teaspoons sea salt
¼ cup oil
1 egg yolk, optional

In a large, warm bowl dissolve yeast with ginger in warm water, stir in molasses, and set aside 5 to 10 minutes until it proves (bubbles).

Mix together flours and salt.

Stir the yeast mixture and add half the flour mixture and the oil. Beat vigorously until smooth, about 10 minutes. Work in remaining flour. Add a little extra whole-wheat flour if dough is too moist.

Divide dough in half and put into 2 well-buttered or oiled 5″x9″ bread pans, cover with a damp cloth, and set aside in a warm place (75°–85°) until double in bulk, about 45 minutes to 1 hour.

Preheat oven to 375°.

Gently brush beaten egg yolk on top of loaves and bake at 375° about 50 minutes or until an inserted toothpick comes out clean.
Yield: 2 loaves

Whole-Wheat Corn Bread

1 cup stone-ground corn meal
½ cup whole-wheat flour
2 tablespoons noninstant nonfat dry milk
2 tablespoons raw wheat germ
2 teaspoons nutritional yeast
2 teaspoons baking powder
1 egg, slightly beaten
1 cup buttermilk
¼ cup melted butter

Preheat oven to 375°.

Combine dry ingredients and sift, returning any particles left in sifter to the bowl.

Combine liquid ingredients.

Stir the dry ingredients a third at a time into liquid ingredients. Pour into a buttered 8-inch square pan or into corn muffin tins and bake at 375° for 30 to 35 minutes or until an inserted toothpick comes out dry.

Cut into squares.
Yield: 16 squares or muffins

Peanut Muffins

¼ cup butter, softened
1 egg
¼ cup 100% peanut butter
2 tablespoons honey
1 cup milk
1 cup whole-wheat pastry flour
¼ cup soy flour
½ teaspoon sea salt
3 teaspoons baking powder
1 tablespoon nutritional yeast
½ cup raw wheat germ
1 cup whole raw peanuts

Preheat oven to 375°.

In a large bowl, beat butter and egg; the butter will be in small pieces. Beat in peanut butter, honey, and milk.

In a separate bowl sift flours, salt, and baking powder, returning any particles left in sifter to the bowl. Stir in yeast and wheat germ.

Add dry ingredients to liquid ingredients, stirring only long enough to combine, and add the peanuts.

Spoon into well-buttered or -oiled muffin tins. Use a large 12-cup muffin tin or medium-sized 12- and 6-cup muffin tins. Fill cups ⅔ full and bake at 375° 20 to 25 minutes or until an inserted toothpick comes out clean.

Yield: 12–18 muffins

Note: Any nut butters and nuts may be used, such as walnuts and cashews. Sesame seeds may also be used with sesame butter, or tahini as it is called, which may be purchased at a natural food store.

Orange Muffins

1½ cups whole-wheat flour
½ cup soy flour
1 teaspoon grated orange peel
1 teaspoon sea salt
2 teaspoons baking powder
1 egg, slightly beaten
2 tablespoons soy oil
¼ cup honey
¼ cup unsweetened frozen orange juice concentrate
¼ cup milk

Preheat oven to 375°.

Combine ingredients in order given and stir only slightly; the batter will be lumpy.

Spoon into buttered muffin tins and bake at 375° for 18 to 20 minutes or until browned.

Yield: 12 muffins

Wheat Germ Muffins

3 cups raw wheat germ
½ cup soy flour, sifted
½ cup rice polish, sifted
1 teaspoon sea salt
2 teaspoons baking powder
1 teaspoon grated lemon peel
2 eggs, beaten
1 tablespoon melted butter or oil
2 tablespoons honey
2 cups milk
Juice of 1 lemon

Preheat oven to 375°.

In a large bowl combine wheat germ, soy flour, rice polish, salt, baking powder, and grated lemon peel.

Combine beaten eggs with butter or oil, honey, milk, and lemon juice. Add to the dry mixture, blending well.

Pour into buttered or oiled muffin pan, filling cups ⅔ full, and bake at 375° for 35 minutes or until an inserted toothpick comes out clean.

Yield: 12 muffins

Raisin–Bran Muffins

1½ pounds bran flakes
2¼ quarts milk
3 cups unsulphured molasses
6 eggs
⅓ cup melted butter
1 pound 2 ounces whole-wheat pastry flour
2 tablespoons baking powder
1 tablespoon sea salt
1½ pounds raisins

Preheat oven to 375°.

Combine bran, milk, and molasses in a large bowl and let stand for 15 minutes.

Add eggs and butter and beat at medium speed for just 1 minute.

Mix flour, baking powder, salt, and raisins. Add to mixture all at once. Beat at low speed just long enough to blend.

Measure out with a #16 dipper and put into muffin pans. Bake at 375° for 15 to 20 minutes or until an inserted toothpick comes out dry.
Yield: 60 muffins

Apples

Fresh Fruit Muffins

¾ cup rye flour
3 teaspoons baking powder
1 teaspoon sea salt
1 cup raw wheat germ
2 eggs
⅓ cup butter, softened
1 cup milk
2 tablespoons unsulphured molasses
1 cup fresh berries or cut-up peaches, pears,
   apricots, or apples

Preheat oven to 375°.

Sift together flour, baking powder, and salt. Stir in wheat germ.

Beat together eggs, butter, milk, and molasses.

Stir dry ingredients into liquid mixture and stir in fruit.

Pour into buttered muffin pan and bake at 375° for 25 minutes or until an inserted toothpick comes out clean.
Yield: 12 muffins

Popovers

1 cup rye flour
½ teaspoon sea salt
1 cup milk
4 eggs
Softened butter or oil

Preheat oven to 500°.

Use cast-iron popover pans for best results; put them in the oven while it is preheating.

Sift flour and salt together.

In another bowl beat eggs, then beat in milk. Then stir in flour quickly.

Remove popover pan from oven (closing oven door), brush butter or oil into popover pan quickly, and pour in batter ⅔ full.

Bake at 500° for 10 minutes. Reduce heat to 425° and bake 15 minutes longer. Prick popovers to let out steam and leave in oven a moment longer.

Yield: 10 popovers

Note: If whole-wheat flour is used in place of rye flour, add ¼ cup more milk to the recipe.

Whole-Wheat Biscuits

2 cups whole-wheat pastry flour
3 teaspoons baking powder
½ teaspoon sea salt
4 tablespoons cold butter
1 egg, slightly beaten
¾ cup milk

Preheat oven to 400°.

Sift together flour, baking powder, and salt, returning any particles left in sifter to the bowl.

Cut butter into dry ingredients with knives or work in quickly with fingertips.

Add egg and milk and mix together. Add a little more milk or more flour if needed for consistency to pat out lightly on floured board to ½-inch thickness.

Cut with 2-inch biscuit cutter and place on buttered baking sheet. For crisp biscuits, place them apart on the baking sheet; place them close together for soft biscuits.

Bake at 400° for 10 to 12 minutes or until browned.
Yield: 20 medium biscuits

Note: For drop biscuits, add enough milk to make a wet dough and drop by tablespoon onto buttered baking sheet and bake as above.

Rye Biscuits

3¼ cups whole-rye flour
3 teaspoons baking powder
½ cup safflower oil
2 eggs
1 cup sour cream

Preheat oven to 400°.

Sift dry ingredients, returning any particles left in sifter to bowl.

Beat eggs slightly with a whisk, whisk in oil and sour cream.

Add the egg mixture to the flour, mixing lightly.

Flour hands and turn dough out onto lightly floured board. Pat, or roll, to ¼ inch thickness.

Cut desired size with biscuit cutter, place on lightly oiled baking sheet. For crisp biscuits, place them apart on baking sheet; for soft biscuits place them close together.

Bake at 400° for 10 to 12 minutes or until browned.
Yield: 24 2-inch biscuits

Buttermilk–Rice Drop Biscuits

¾ cup brown rice flour
¼ cup soy flour
2 teaspoons baking powder
½ teaspoon sea salt
2 tablespoons cold butter
1 egg
½ cup (approximately) buttermilk

Preheat oven to 400°.

Sift together flours, baking powder, and salt.

Cut butter into dry ingredients, or work in with fingertips.

In a separate bowl, stir egg into ⅓ cup of the buttermilk and add gradually to dry ingredients. Add enough extra buttermilk to make a wet dough and drop by tablespoons on a buttered baking sheet.

Bake at 400° for 12 to 15 minutes or until done. The biscuits will be light in color.
Yield: 12 biscuits

Apple Muffins

English muffins (whole-grain)
Apples, peeled, cored, and thinly sliced
Melted butter
Honey
Powdered ginger
Nutmeg

Preheat oven to 400°.

With a fork, carefully tear English muffins in halves; allow 1 to 2 halves for each serving.

Brush muffins with melted butter.

Top each half with 5 or 6 very thin apple slices that have been dipped in melted butter.

Drizzle each half with a little honey and sprinkle on a dash of powdered ginger and nutmeg.

Bake at 400° for 15 minutes or until apples are just tender.

Apple Coffeecake

1½ cups whole-wheat pastry flour
1½ cups brown rice flour
¼ cup soy flour
¼ cup nonfat dry milk
4 teaspoons baking powder
1 teaspoon sea salt
2 teaspoons nutmeg
¼ cup raw wheat germ
4 eggs, beaten
½ cup honey
½ cup safflower oil
¾ cup milk
1 teaspoon pure vanilla extract
3 apples peeled, cored, and thinly sliced

Preheat oven to 350°.

Sift together flours, dry milk, baking powder, salt, and nutmeg. Stir in wheat germ.

Combine eggs, honey, oil, milk, and vanilla. Stir into dry ingredients.

Pour ⅓ of the batter into a well-buttered 9″x9″ baking pan and spread ⅓ of the apple slices over it. Pour half of the remaining batter over the apples and place half of the remaining apple slices over the batter. Pour the rest of the batter over the apples and top with rows of sliced apples.

Bake at 350° for 45 to 50 minutes or until an inserted toothpick comes out clean.
Serves 8

Puris (East Indian Bread)

1¼ cups whole-wheat flour
½ teaspoon sea salt
½ teaspoon ground cumin seed
½ teaspoon turmeric
1 teaspoon ginger powder
¼ cup softened butter
¾ cup yogurt
Safflower oil

Combine flour, seasonings, butter, and yogurt.

Roll out ¹⁄₁₆″ or as thin as possible on a floured board. Cut into 2¼″ rounds.

Heat oil ½″ deep over medium heat until a small piece of the dough fries instantly.

Drop in one by one and cook briefly, a minute or less, holding down with a slotted spoon, until puffy and brown. Drain on a paper towel.
Yield: 12

Steamed Brown Bread

1¾ cups rye bread crumbs
7 cups cold water
1½ cups unsulphured molasses
1 pound stone-ground corn meal
1 pound plus ½ cup rye flour
2 tablespoons baking powder
2 teaspoons sea salt

Soak bread crumbs in water for 1 hour and add molasses.

Combine corn meal, flour, baking powder, and salt and add to crumbs and molasses.

Divide into 8 brown-bread or coffee cans, cover, and steam for 3 hours.
Yield: 64 slices

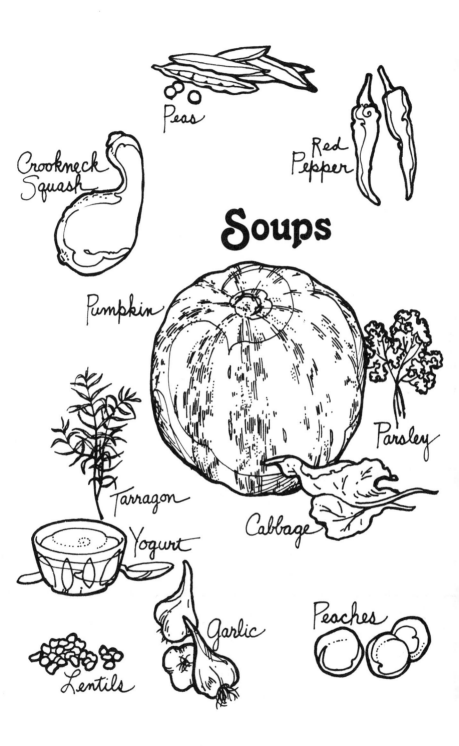

Peas

Red Pepper

Crookneck Squash

Soups

Pumpkin

Parsley

Tarragon

Yogurt

Cabbage

Garlic

Lentils

Peaches

No dish brings better nutrition or greater satisfaction than a steaming bowl of fragrant homemade soup. Furthermore, it may serve as a complete meal with only the addition of a slice of whole-grain bread or a muffin and some fresh fruit for dessert. Homemade soups are economical and are not difficult to prepare. In fact, they are fun because, as the saying goes, almost everything in the kitchen can go into the soup pot—and this includes all kinds of good scraps and leftovers one hates to throw out, but which, in themselves, are not enough for a meal.

The most convincing evidence that soup should be made at home is printed on the cans and packages of the commercial soups on your supermarket shelves. When you look them over, you will not doubt that an estimated 20,000 tons of MSG (monosodium glutamate) are poured into commercial soups every year in the United States. One look at the additives and sugar listed on the labels of commercial soups will make you immune to the deception of advertising. It will also tell you what you have been eating and what is served in the majority of restaurants and hospitals. But, happily, the labels will also drive you to making your own soups from scratch.

There are many advantages to homemade soup besides avoiding additives and sugar; you can bring to your soups all kinds of healthy ingredients that are not incorporated in commercial products.

For the most part, soups can be dreamed up as you go along. All you need is a good heavy saucepan or soup kettle and a little imagination. There are two basic methods of making homemade stocks.

The first is to save the water in which vegetables and potatoes are cooked. Collect it in a large jar or two and keep refrigerated. Include in this collection the water in which you have soaked beans, peas, grains, and seeds before cooking or sprouting. Also save any juices from meat and the water in which meat, fish, or poultry have been cooked. Then use these ready-made stocks as the base for your own soup recipe. Simply add any vegetables you wish and simmer the soup for a few minutes. Or add leftovers and heat through. And, if you wish, add cooked brown rice, potatoes, whole-grain noodles, eggs (raw or hard-boiled), nuts, or seeds. Whole grains may be added to soups by grinding them first for quick cooking. Add whatever sprouts you have at the end of the cooking period. Season to your own taste with fresh lemon juice, kelp, tamari sauce, or sea salt.

The second method is to make special stocks. These meat, poultry, and fish stocks are also easily made at home and are a great convenience to have on hand for soups, sauces, and various dishes. Simply cover meat, fowl, or fish, and bones with cold water and bring to a boil. Turn heat down and simmer, skimming off any scum that forms the first few minutes. Then add any, or all, of the following: a carrot, celery stalk, onion, and herb (marjoram, basil, thyme, etc.). Simmer 2 to 3 hours and strain. If flavor is not strong enough, reduce stock by half by boiling rapidly. Cool, refrigerate, and remove any fat which will surface and harden. Pour into jars or ice cube trays and store for future use.

Cream soups are quickly and easily made. In blender place raw or partially cooked vegetables with a little water or with the water in which they were cooked. Blend until smooth and add enough milk, cream, or yogurt to obtain the desired consistency. Heat through and season as desired.

Crookneck
Squash

Beef Broth

6 pounds shin and marrow bones, cut up
1½ pounds beef chuck, cut up
4 quarts water
3 celery stalks, cut up
1 carrot, cut up
1 onion, cut in half
1 bay leaf
3 sprigs parsley
1 teaspoon thyme
8 black peppercorns
1 tablespoon sea salt

Place beef bones and meat in an uncovered soup kettle and cover with cold water. Bring to a boil, reduce heat, and simmer 10 minutes, removing scum as it rises to the surface.

Add remaining ingredients and put lid on kettle with edge of lid slightly off on one side to allow steam to escape. Simmer about 3 hours or until reduced by half. If flavor is not strong enough, reduce broth further by rapid boiling.

Strain through a fine strainer or 2 thicknesses of cheese-cloth wrung out in water. Cool in refrigerator and skim off any fat which surfaces. Cut meat off bones and return to broth.

Reheat before serving and taste for seasoning. It may need a little more sea salt. Cut-up vegetables may be added and simmered a few minutes before serving.

Yield: About 2 quarts

Tips: To have beef stock on hand for further use in recipes, make twice the amount and, before adding meat to finished broth, pour half of it into ice-cube trays. Freeze and store the cubes for later use.

If a darker brown and fuller-flavored stock is desired, brown the meat and bones in the oven before starting the soup.

Chicken Broth

1 large stewing chicken, or 4 pounds of
    chicken backs, necks, and wings
4 cups water
1 bay leaf
Optional:
    1 teaspoon thyme
    2 celery stalks, cut up
    1 carrot, cut up
    8 peppercorns

Place chicken in soup kettle and cover with cold water. Add a bay leaf and other ingredients, if desired. Simmer with cover slightly off at one side for 1 hour for whole chicken and 2 hours if only the backs, necks, and wings are used.

Remove chicken from pot and season broth with sea salt to taste. If chicken parts are used, strain broth, return to pot, and season with sea salt.

If a stronger broth is desired, it may be reduced by rapid boiling.

Freeze the broth not in use in ice-cube trays and store for future use in recipes calling for chicken broth, such as sauces.

Use stewed chicken as desired for salads, sandwiches, and chicken dishes. Add a little chicken, cut up, and whatever meat has fallen off bones to broth before serving. Cooked brown rice may be added to the broth.

Yield: About 2 quarts

Carrots

Chicken Jambalaya

1 3½ to 4½ pound chicken, cut up
Safflower oil
1 onion, chopped
1 green pepper, chopped
3 celery stalks, chopped
6 cups water
3 cups brown rice
2 tablespoons chopped parsley
1 teaspoon rosemary
½ teaspoon sea salt
¼ teaspoon pepper

In a heavy pot, brown chicken pieces in oil. Add onion, pepper, and celery and cook briefly until onion is transparent.

Add water and remaining ingredients. Bring to a boil, reduce heat, and simmer for 1 hour or until water is absorbed and rice is fluffy.

Serves 3–4

Gulyas Soup (Goulash Soup)

2 pounds beef chuck or round steak
Whole-wheat flour
Safflower oil
6 cups water, beef stock, or tomato juice
1 onion, chopped
2 green peppers, chopped
2 carrots cut in ½-inch slices
2 celery stalks, cut in ½-inch slices
8 small potatoes, scrubbed
1 tablespoon paprika
1 teaspoon sea salt

Cut beef into 1-inch cubes, dip in flour, and brown on all sides in oil in a heavy soup pot.

Add water (or stock or juice), bones, and onion. Simmer for 1½ hours.

Remove bones from pot, add vegetables and seasonings, and simmer 30 minutes longer. Serve hot.
Serves 8

Peas

Cream of Pumpkin Soup

1 pumpkin (about 2½ pounds)
2 cups water
½ teaspoon cinnamon
½ teaspoon ground coriander
½ teaspoon allspice
1 quart milk
Sea salt and pepper to taste

Peel, seed, and clean pumpkin and cut into large cubes.

In a soup kettle place pumpkin, water, cinnamon, coriander, and allspice. Simmer until pumpkin is tender.

Put pumpkin in blender or force through a strainer. Add milk and simmer slowly 10 minutes. Season to taste.
Serves 6

Quick Vegetable Soup

1 cup spinach leaves or broccoli, asparagus, cauliflower, beans, peas, corn kernels, etc.
½ cup yogurt
½ teaspoon sea salt
¼ cup cream or milk
Thin lemon slices

Cook vegetable briefly (2 to 4 minutes).

Place vegetable, yogurt, salt, and cream or milk in blender.

Blend until smooth.

Serve either hot or cold. Garnish with lemon slices.
Serves 2

Oat Soup

6 cups beef or chicken broth (pages 156, 157)
¼ cup rolled oats
2 tablespoons butter

Bring broth to a boil, add oats, and cook until done. Add the butter and serve.
Serves 6

Cabbage–Rice Soup

2 cups shredded cabbage
3 cups beef or chicken broth (pages 156, 157)
2 tablespoons butter
½ cup cooked brown rice
½ cup grated Parmesan cheese

Cook cabbage in a little boiling water for 5 minutes and drain.

Combine cabbage with rice and cheese.

Heat broth, add cabbage mixture, and serve.
Serves 6

Cold Avocado Soup

2 large or 3 small avocados, peeled and cut up
3 cups yogurt
3 tablespoons minced onion
¼ cup lemon juice
1 teaspoon sea salt
Fresh mint or lemon wedges with parsley garnish

Combine all ingredients and put in blender. Blend until smooth and chill.

Pour into chilled soup cups and garnish with fresh mint or lemon wedges dipped in chopped parsley.
Serves 4

Cabbage

Peanut Butter Soup

1½ tablespoons whole-wheat flour
3 tablespoons butter
6 tablespoons 100-percent peanut butter
3 cups milk
Sea salt

Melt butter in a saucepan and add the flour. Simmer 3 minutes.

Stir in peanut butter and heat through.

Add milk, stirring, and cook until hot.

Salt slightly and serve.
Serves 4

South African Curry Soup

1 onion, chopped
Oil
6 cups beef broth with meat (page 156)
2 bay leaves, crushed
2 tablespoons curry powder (or to taste)
2 potatoes, sliced
2 tablespoons apple cider vinegar
2 teaspoons sea salt

Cook onion in a little oil until transparent.

Combine onion, broth with meat, bay leaves, and curry powder; simmer for 5 minutes.

Add potatoes, vinegar, and salt and simmer until potatoes are tender.
Serves 6

Chicken–Peanut Soup

1 stewing chicken and broth (page 157)
½ cup 100% peanut butter
2 teaspoons tomato paste
Sea salt
2 tablespoons chopped parsley

Cook broth until reduced to 8 cups. Remove ½ cup and mix with peanut butter; return to broth.

Cut up 2 cups chicken and add to broth with tomato paste and salt to taste.

Serve sprinkled with chopped parsley.
Serves 8

Hawaiian Chicken Broth

6 cups chicken broth (page 157)
1 garlic clove, crushed
¼ teaspoon ginger powder
1 cup cubed papaya, avocado, or melon

Heat broth with seasonings, pour into soup cups, and float fruit cubes.
Serves 6

Barley or Brown Rice Soup

1 cup barley or brown rice
4 cups water
1 onion, chopped
½ cup diced celery
Safflower oil
1 cup peas
Sea salt

Place barley or rice in water in soup kettle and simmer 1 hour.

Sauté onions and celery in oil until transparent and add to barley or rice with peas and salt. Simmer 10 minutes longer.
Serves 4

Note: This soup may be made with any flaked grain, and other vegetables may be added, such as, carrots, tomatoes, mushrooms, green beans, etc. It may also be made with vegetable water or chicken broth instead of water.

Chicken Broth With Sprouts

1 teaspoon powdered ginger
1½ teaspoons sea salt
2½ quarts chicken broth (page 157)
1 cup bean sprouts
1 cup water chestnuts, sliced
3 hard-boiled eggs
2 cups cooked chicken in slivers
Lemon slices

Combine ginger and salt with broth and simmer 3 minutes.

Add sprouts, chestnuts, eggs, and chicken and simmer 2 more minutes.

Pour into soup dishes and garnish with lemon slices.
Serves 6

Curried Lentil Soup

½ cup lentils
6 cups water
½ cup chopped onions
Sesame oil
1 tablespoon curry powder
1 tablespoon lemon juice
Sea salt

Cook lentils in boiling water for 1 hour.

Sauté onions in oil until transparent; add curry powder and sauté 1 minute longer.

Add onions and curry to pot with lentils and simmer 10 minutes.

Add lemon juice and salt to taste.

Serve this way or put into blender until smooth.
Serves 6

Cheese Soup

2 teaspoons minced onion
2 tablespoons butter
2 tablespoons whole-wheat flour
3 cups beef broth, warm
1 cup milk, scalded
1 cup grated Cheddar cheese
Sea salt

Sauté the onions in butter, add flour, and simmer 3 minutes.

Add beef broth slowly, stirring, and simmer 3 more minutes.

Add the milk, stirring, and then the cheese, blending well, but cook only until cheese is melted. Season to taste.
Serves 4

Vegetable Beef Soup

15 pounds beef shank with meat
4 gallons cold water
3 bay leaves, crushed
3 tablespoons sea salt
1½ pounds carrots, scrubbed and cubed
2 pounds celery, scrubbed and chopped
2 pounds peas
2 pounds cut green beans
2 pounds onions, chopped
Sea salt and pepper

Combine beef, water, bay leaves, and salt and bring to boiling point. Turn down heat and simmer 3 hours.

Remove shanks from soup, chop meat, and set aside.

Add vegetables to soup and simmer 15 minutes. Add chopped meat, and salt and pepper if needed.
Yield: 3 gallons or 48 1-cup servings

Tomato Broth

8 tomatoes, peeled and chopped
1 medium onion, chopped
1 cup chopped celery
1 cup chicken broth (page 157)
1 teaspoon sea salt
1 tablespoon nutritional yeast (optional)
Chopped chives

Simmer all ingredients, except chives, 10 minutes. Put in blender and blend until smooth.

Serve hot or cold. Garnish with chopped chives.
Serves 4

Bean Soup

5 pounds garbanzo beans (chick peas) or kidney beans
4½ gallons boiling water
1 pound onions, chopped
1½ gallons tomato puree (without additives)
¼ cup kelp granules
2 tablespoons sea salt
Whole-wheat croutons (page 166)

Wash beans and add boiling water; cover and let stand 1 hour. Cook in the same water until beans are tender.

Purée in blender and add enough water to measure 1½ gallons.

Heat tomato purée, add kelp and salt, and add to bean purée. Simmer 5 minutes, stirring, to blend the soup.

Serve with whole-wheat croutons.
Yield: 3 gallons or 48 1-cup servings

Cheddar Cheese

Celeriac

Garnishes for Soups

Puffed brown rice, whole wheat, or millet
Seeds: sesame, sunflower, or pumpkin
Lemon or lime slices
Thin cucumber slices
Thin hard-boiled egg slices
Omelet cut into strips
Sprouts
Minced parsley
Chopped chives
Chopped celery leaves
Chopped mint leaves
Herbs: thyme, marjoram, basil, etc.
Slivered, toasted nuts
Toasted soybeans
Wheat germ
Nasturtium or peony petals
Grated cheese
Whole-grain bread or cracker crumbs
Whole-grain croutons

Croutons

Whole-grain bread slices
Butter

Cut whole-grain bread slices into small cubes and combine with melted butter.

Place on baking sheet and bake at 400° until toasted on all sides. Stir frequently.

Borscht

3 large or 4 medium beets, shredded
4 cups beef broth with meat (page 156)
1 tablespoon butter
1 tablespoon honey
2 teaspoons cider vinegar
Sea salt
Sour cream

Blend two-thirds of the shredded beets with the broth and meat in blender until smooth.

Combine the remaining portion of shredded beets with the blended mixture and simmer until beets are tender but still crisp.

Add butter, honey, and vinegar. Season with salt.

Pour into soup dishes and top with a good dab of sour cream.
Serves 6

Note: Sour cream may be stirred into soup before serving, if preferred.

Beets

Fruit Soup

4 cups fruit (berries or cut-up fruit, such as, apples,
    peaches, apricots, pears, plums, etc.)
4 cups water
Honey to taste, if needed
½ stick cinnamon, optional
¼ cup nut halves, optional
1–2 cups yogurt
Toasted wheat germ

Put fruit in blender a cup at a time with a little water and blend
until smooth. Pour into a saucepan.

Add remaining water, honey (if needed), and cinnamon stick.
Simmer 15 minutes, stirring occasionally with a wooden spoon.

Remove cinnamon stick and add nuts, if desired.

Serve hot or cold with yogurt on top and sprinkled with wheat
germ.
Serves 6

Salads and Salad Dressings

Leeks

Blue Cheese

Olives

Celeriac

Endive

Red Cabbage

Apples

Shrimp

Sunflower Seeds

We can live, and live well, on salads because they encompass all aspects of nutrition—vegetables, fruits, grains, meat, poultry, fish, seafood, cheese, eggs, nuts, seeds, gelatins, and many other nutritious ingredients.

All vitamins, minerals, and other food factors are available to us in raw food, especially if it has been grown in good soil and is properly handled after harvesting. This includes washing greens immediately by immersing them in cold water, then drying and refrigerating them. The longer greens are left out in the light at room temperature, the more vitamin and mineral content they lose. The most satisfactory way of drying greens is the French way—in a wire basket. The wet greens are placed in the basket, then the basket is shaken, twirled, or gaily flung back and forth French-fashion while the excess moisture is dispersed. Salad greens may also be shaken in a towel, or they may be dried by patting with cloth or paper toweling.

Greens should be stored in the refrigerator to be kept crisp. In recent years, plastic bags have served as the most convenient means of storing greens, but I am giving up the use of plastics until further tests by scientists, independent of the plastic industry, have proven them to be safe. The evidence that the gases released in their manufacture may cause cancer among workers, and the suspicion that plastic material may have a toxic effect (although less) in contact with other things, has persuaded me to go back to the old methods for storing food. Unfortunately, technology is moving and being accepted faster than science is able to assess the actual effects of its developments upon humans. Therefore, until we know more, I recommend wrapping your greens in a towel and placing them in a refrigerator drawer.

The beauty of salads lies in the dramatic contrasts of nature's vivid colors and fascinating textures, so there is no trick at all to making a salad attractive. Almost all tender young vegetables may be tossed into a salad raw and many of them whole; these include such vegetables as beets, beet greens, corn kernels, peas, green beans, cauliflower, broccoli, squash, and other vegetables we usually think of cooking before eating. The household with its own vegetable garden has a tremendous advantage.

There are many kinds of lettuce from which to choose. As a rule, the dark green leaves contain the most vitamins and minerals. Use all kinds of lettuce, alone or in combinations: leaf, russet, butter, head, romaine, endive, escarole, and bibb. Use other greens, too, such as green and red cabbage, bok choy, spinach, chard, watercress, dandelion, mustard, collard, vegetable tops and leaves, comfrey leaves, sorrel, kale, and parsley. I would like to emphasize the use of parsley because of its high nutritive value. Perhaps it is for this reason that parsley has been used so extensively through the ages in Europe, especially in the Middle East. Use it generously in salads and in large clumps as a garnish for other dishes. Parsley keeps well in a jar in the refrigerator.

Sprouts are high on the list for use in salads because of the concentration of their nutritive properties: their unique flavors and extra crisp texture also do a great deal for any dish (See page 197 for growing instructions.)

Salad dressings may add to the healthfulness of your salads by supplying unrefined oils, and oils with the least amount of processing, lemon juice, cider and wine vinegars, garlic, herbs, egg yolks, cheese, yogurt, and seeds of all kinds. If you read the labels on the salad dressings in your supermarkets with their large assortment of chemicals, including imitation ingredients, you will want to make your own salad dressings. Aside from the good nutrition homemade salad dressings contribute to a salad, they are easy to make and far more economical.

Whenever you can, add some of the following to your salads for extra nutrition, flavor, and texture:

    Toasted sesame and sunflower seeds
    Pumpkin seeds
    Nuts, ground, chopped or whole
    Roasted soybeans
    Wheat germ
    Kelp powder
    Cheese, crumbled, grated, or cubed
    Hard-boiled eggs, chopped or sliced
    Sprouts

To your dressings add:

>   Nutritional yeast
>   Yogurt
>   Cheese
>   Seeds

The following list of suggested combinations for salads comes from all over the world. Some are quite unusual: be adventuresome and try them.

Vegetable Salads

Bean Sprout and Spinach Salad

1 cup mung bean sprouts
3 cups spinach
¼ cup sliced water chestnuts
2 tablespoons minced onion
3 tablespoons sesame seeds
½ cup sesame seed oil
¼ cup tamari soy sauce
2 tablespoons lemon juice

Combine sprouts, spinach, chestnuts, onion, and sesame seeds. Toss with oil, soy sauce, and lemon juice mixture.
Serves 4

Bean and Alfalfa Sprout Salad

1 cup mung bean sprouts
1 cup alfalfa sprouts
½ cup chopped parsley
½ cup thinly sliced cucumber with peel
1 cup watercress
2 tablespoons thinly sliced green onion
2 large tomatoes, chopped
2 cups romaine lettuce

Toss with oil and lemon dressing.
Serves 6

Bean Sprout and Mushroom Salad

3 cups mung bean sprouts or other sprouts
1 cup sliced fresh mushrooms
¼ cup chopped parsley
1 clove garlic, crushed
1½ cups bamboo shoots
2 tablespoons sesame seeds

Mix above with:

¼ cup peanut or sesame oil
2 tablespoons lemon juice
¼ teaspoon sea salt
⅛ teaspoon grated ginger

Serves 4

Bean Sprout and Broccoli Salad

2 cups mung bean sprouts
1 cup sliced broccoli stems and flowerets
1 cup sliced celery

Mix above with:

3 tablespoons sesame oil
1½ tablespoons tamari soy sauce
1 teaspoon honey

Serves 4

Apple Cider Vinegar

Four Bean Salad

2 pounds green and wax beans
1 cup oil
¼ cup vinegar
1 garlic clove, crushed
1 pound pinto beans
1½ pounds red kidney beans

Cook green and wax beans and marinate in oil and vinegar. Pour boiling water over pinto beans and soak for 3 hours, then cook until tender. Combine all beans with 1 cup oil, ¼ cup vinegar, and garlic. Refrigerate in covered glass container and use as needed.
Serves 12

Five Bean Salad

4 cups kidney beans
1 15-ounce can garbanzo beans
1 package frozen cut wax beans
1 package frozen lima beans
1 package frozen cut green beans

Mix above with:

1 cup oil
½ cup wine vinegar
1½ teaspoons sea salt
1 teaspoon celery seed
1 teaspoon basil

Refrigerate in covered glass container and use as needed.
Serves 20 to 24

174 / *The Real Food Cookbook*

Kidney Bean Salad

4 cups cooked kidney beans
1 onion, finely chopped
1 cucumber, diced with peel on
2 stalks celery, diced
4 hard-boiled eggs, chopped

Mix above with:

½ cup mayonnaise
¼ teaspoon dry mustard
½ teaspoon honey

Serves 8

Green Bean and Sunflower Seed Salad

2 cups green beans
1 teaspoon minced onion
2 tablespoons chopped green pepper
2 tablespoons sunflower seeds

Mix above with:

3 tablespoons sunflower oil
1 tablespoon apple cider vinegar
¼ teaspoon nutmeg
¼ teaspoon sea salt
⅛ teaspoon freshly ground pepper

Serves 2

Green Bean–Pimiento Salad

8 cups cut green beans
2 tablespoons minced onion
2 chopped pimientos
¼ cup chopped parsley

Mix above with:

½ cup oil
¼ cup lemon juice
Sea salt
Freshly ground pepper

Serves 8

Endive

Endive and Beet Salad

1 pound endive, cut up
3 cooked beets, grated
¼ cup safflower oil
1 tablespoon lemon juice
¼ teaspoon mustard powder
1 egg, grated
2 tablespoons chopped chives

Combine endive and beets. Chill. Mix oil, lemon juice, and mustard. Toss endive and beets with dressing and sprinkle with grated egg mixed with chives.
Serves 4

Beet and Orange Salad

12 lettuce leaves
4 large oranges
6 cooked beets
¾ cup unrefined olive oil
¼ cup cider vinegar
¼ teaspoon sea salt
⅛ teaspoon freshly ground pepper
2 teaspoons chopped parsley
2 teaspoons green olives, chopped fine

Arrange 4 orange slices and 3 beet slices on lettuce leaf. Pour over them some of the dressing made from the other ingredients.
Serves 12

Vegetable Salad

3 pounds cut green beans
1 cup sliced carrots
1 cup sliced celery heart
2 pounds peas
1 cup sliced raw mushrooms
Garlic
4 tablespoons chopped chives
4 tablespoons chopped parsley

Steam beans, carrots, celery, and peas together over hot water for 5 minutes. Chill. Add raw mushrooms. Rub a salad bowl with split garlic. Toss vegetables in bowl with:

1 cup unrefined olive oil
½ cup tarragon vinegar
2 teaspoons sea salt
½ teaspoon pepper

Sprinkle with chives and parsley.
Serves 24

Tabooley

1 cup fine cracked wheat
3 cups water
2 large bunches parsley
1 bunch mint
6 green onions
3 tomatoes
½ cup unrefined olive oil
¼ cup lemon juice
½ teaspoon sea salt
Grape leaves or romaine

Soak wheat in water for a few mintues and squeeze dry. Remove stems from parsley and mint. Chop fine with onions and tomatoes and mix with olive oil, lemon juice, and salt. Serve on grape leaves or romaine. (In the Near East they use grape leaves as scoops with which to eat the salads).
Serves 8

Red and White Coleslaw

1 head red cabbage
1 head white cabbage
6 green onions, chopped
1 tablespoon chopped parsley
½ pineapple, chopped (optional)
⅔ cup safflower oil
½ cup lemon juice
2 tablespoons celery or caraway seed
1 teaspoon kelp powder

Shred cabbage. Add other ingredients.
Serves 12

Coleslaw for Fifty

5 pounds cabbage, shredded
1½ pounds carrots, shredded
5 cups unsweetened crushed pineapple (optional)

Mix with:

1½ quarts sour cream or yogurt
1½ tablespoons sea salt
1½ cups vinegar
½ cup honey

Serves 50

Cabbage and Yogurt Salad

1 head (2 pounds) red or white cabbage
1 green pepper, chopped
2 green onions, chopped
¼ teaspoon caraway or celery seed

Shred cabbage and combine with other ingredients. Mix with
dressing made of:

¼ cup yogurt
¼ cup mayonnaise
Sea salt, if desired

Serves 8

Dandelion Salad

1 quart torn-up dandelion leaves (picked before
    blossoms form)
1 tablespoon chopped onion or shallots
2 tablespoons parsley
1 cup watercress
2 tablespoons wheat germ
1 tablespoon toasted sesame seeds
½ teaspoon summer savory
Garlic

Rub a salad bowl with split garlic clove, put vegetables in bowl, and toss with dressing made of:

¼ cup sesame oil
2 tablespoons lemon juice

Serves 6

Eggplant Salad

1 large eggplant
½ cup minced onion
¼ cup lemon juice
1 teaspoon honey
1 teaspoon sea salt
1 garlic clove, crushed
1 teaspoon basil
Freshly ground pepper
1 tablespoon unrefined olive oil
Sliced tomatoes
Chopped parsley

Wash eggplant and poke holes into it with a fork. Place on a baking dish in a 400° oven for 1 hour. Cool, peel, and chop fine. Combine with onion, lemon juice, honey, sea salt, garlic, basil, and a little freshly ground pepper. Chill. To serve, add 1 table-spoon unrefined olive oil and pile in center of a platter. Surround with sliced tomatoes sprinkled with chopped parsley.
Serves 4

Avocado and Spinach Salad

4 avocados, sliced
8 cups chopped raw spinach leaves
Nutmeg
4 hard-boiled eggs, chopped
2 tablespoons minced onion

Arrange avocado slices on spinach leaves. Sprinkle with nutmeg, egg, and onion, and drizzle over it the following dressing:

½ cup all-blend or safflower oil
2 tablespoons tarragon vinegar
1 teaspoon sea salt
¼ teaspoon pepper
2 teaspoons chopped parsley

Serves 8

Spinach and Mushroom Salad

Torn-up spinach
Sliced water chestnuts
Sliced raw mushrooms

Mix with oil and vinegar dressing.

Tossed Salads

Use any desired dressing for these.

Spinach and Peanut Salad

2 avocados, sliced
10 ounces spinach, torn-up
½ pound bacon (without additives), cooked crisp
  and crumbled (optional)
½ cup peanuts or pumpkin seeds

Serves 4

Spinach

Pea and Tomato Salad

1 cup green peas
1 green pepper, chopped
4 green onions, chopped
2 stalks celery, chopped
2 tomatoes, peeled, seeded, and chopped

Serves 2

Vegetable and Sunflower Seed Salad

½ cup peas
½ cup asparagus tips
½ cup cut green beans
6 artichoke hearts
½ cup sunflower seeds

Steam peas, asparagus, and beans together over boiling water for 4 minutes. Cool and add artichoke hearts and seeds.
Serves 2

Garden Salad

1 cup new green peas
8 small new carrots
Corn kernels from 2 ears
4 celery stalks, chopped with leaves
4 new tiny beets
1 bunch parsley, chopped
2 hard-boiled eggs, chopped
½ cup sprouts
½ bunch lettuce
½ cup walnut or pecan halves

Serves 6

Tossed Salad for Fifty

6 pounds lettuce, torn-up
1 pound cucumber, sliced with peel
1½ pounds celery, diced
½ pound carrots, sliced
50 watercress sprigs
3 bunches parsley
6 pounds tomatoes, peeled and cut in eighths
12 hard-boiled eggs, chopped
10 green peppers sliced into rings
8 ounces combined grated Romano and Parmesan cheese

Toss with dressing made of:

1½ pints safflower oil
¼ pint cider vinegar
1 tablespoon sea salt
1 teaspoon pepper
4 garlic cloves, crushed

Serves 50

Fruit Salads

Fruit and Peanut Salad

3 oranges in sections
2 small or 1 large juicamas
or
2 apples, peeled and chopped
2 bananas, sliced
2 cups fresh or unsweetened canned pineapple chunks
½ cup chopped peanuts
1 bunch lettuce, torn-up
½ cup mayonnaise
Pomegranate seeds

Mix all ingredients except last. Sprinkle with pomegranate seeds.
Serves 6

Apple and Watercress Salad

1 avocado, sliced
4 apples, sliced into wedges ¼-inch thick with peel on
1 bunch watercress
¼ cup almond slivers

Toss with oil and lemon juice dressing.
Serves 4

Combination Fruit Salad

1 cantaloupe, sliced
1 cup strawberries
1 cup sliced peaches
1 cup cherries
1 cup sliced pear
1 cup seedless grapes
1 cup sliced orange

Dressing:

½ cup pineapple juice
¼ cup lemon juice
3 eggs, beaten well
2 tablespoons honey
⅛ teaspoon sea salt

Combine dressing ingredients in double boiler and cook over boiling water, stirring, until thick.

Combine all the cups of fruit and pile the combination on top of cantaloupe slices. Pour over each some of the dressing.
Serves 6

Banana Salad

2 bananas
1 cup chopped peanuts
4 lettuce leaves
4 tangerine or tangelo sections
Mayonnaise
Pomegranate, sunflower, or pumpkin seeds

Peel bananas and cut into strips. Roll strips in chopped peanuts.
Arrange on lettuce leaves with tangerine or tangelo sections.
Top with a dab of mayonnaise and sprinkle with seeds.
Serves 4

Cranberry Salad

½ cup cooked cranberries
½ cup chopped celery
¼ cup chopped nuts
Lettuce leaves

Combine cranberries, celery, and nuts and serve on lettuce
leaves with a combination of:
2 tablespoons mayonnaise
2 tablespoons whipping cream
Serves 2

Cranberry–Fruit Gelatin Salad

1 tablespoon pure gelatin
¼ cup pineapple juice
1¼ cups pineapple juice
1 cup raw, ground cranberries
1 orange, chopped
½ cup walnut or pecan halves

Soften gelatin in ¼ cup pineapple juice. Dissolve in 1¼ cups
heated pineapple juice and add cranberries and orange. Add
nuts and pour into oiled mold.
Serves 4–6

Pomegranate

Fruit Gelatin Salad for 4 or 50

Follow recipe on page 226. Cut into four squares, place each square on a large lettuce leaf, and garnish with a tablespoon of mayonnaise.

Serves 4

Follow recipe on page 227. Cut into squares, place on lettuce leaves, and garnish with mayonnaise, using 4 pounds leaf lettuce and 1 quart mayonnaise.

Serves 50

Fruit Salad for 25

3 quarts chopped apples, with peels on
2 quarts diced celery
1 quart seedless grapes
1½ cups chopped walnuts
2½ cups sour cream
¼ cup honey
½ cup cider vinegar
¾ cup mayonnaise
2 pounds lettuce leaves

Make dressing of sour cream, honey, vinegar, and mayonnaise. Add apples to it as soon as they are chopped to keep them from turning brown. Then add other fruits and serve on lettuce leaves.

Serves 25

Avocado

Fowl and Meat Salads

Chicken and Roquefort Salad

½ cup safflower oil or unrefined olive oil
2 tablespoons wine vinegar
2 tablespoons lemon juice
1 teaspoon sea salt
½ teaspoon pepper
1 garlic clove, crushed
1 teaspoon Worcestershire sauce

Make a dressing of the above ingredients. Put in a jar and shake well.

2 heads lettuce torn (preferably 2 different kinds)
3 tablespoons sliced green onions

Toss lettuce with onions and a little of the dressing and arrange on a platter. Fill the center with following ingredients mixed with a little dressing.

2 cups cooked chicken, diced
1 large tomato, diced
½ cup Roquefort or blue cheese

Surround chicken with:

2 avocados, sliced
Sprigs of watercress
2 hard-boiled eggs, quartered

Serves 6

Chicken and Almond Salad

2 cups cooked, diced chicken
1 cup sprouts
1 hard-boiled egg, chopped
¼ cup almond slivers

Brown almond slivers in butter and combine with chicken, sprouts, and egg. Mix with dressing made of:

½ cup sesame oil
2 tablespoons tamari soy sauce
1 teaspoon honey

Serve on lettuce.
Serves 4–6

Elegant Chicken Salad

1 large chicken
1 cup mayonnaise
¼ cup yogurt
1 tablespoon prepared mustard
1 tablespoon lemon juice
Sea salt
Pepper
Paprika
Lettuce leaves
Watercress
Hard-boiled eggs, quartered

Cool chicken and remove meat and dice in large chunks. Combine mayonnaise with yogurt, mustard, lemon juice, salt, pepper, and paprika. Mix with chicken and serve on lettuce leaves. Garnish with watercress and eggs.
Serves 6

Duck and Orange Salad

2 cups cut-up duck
2 oranges, peeled and sliced

Combine and mix with dressing made of:

½ cup unrefined olive oil
2 tablespoons lemon juice
½ teaspoon sea salt
½ teaspoon pepper
¼ teaspoon paprika
½ teaspoon tarragon

Serve on lettuce leaves and garnish with parsley or watercress and additional orange slices.
Serves 3–4

Oranges

Chef Salad with Sprouts

1 or 2 bunches lettuce
1 cup chopped celery
1 green pepper, cut in thin strips
1 Bermuda onion, sliced thin
2 tomatoes, cut in eighths
½ cucumber, sliced thin with peel on
1 cup diced Cheddar cheese
1 cup julienne strips chicken or turkey
1 cup julienne strips beef
½ cup sprouts

Toss with desired dressing and garnish with parsley and hard-boiled egg quarters.
Serves 8

Meat and Vegetable Salad

2 cups beef (or any leftover meat cut into large chunks)
1 cup sliced cooked potatoes
½ cup cooked cut green beans
1 cup chopped watercress or parsley
1 tablespoon chopped chives

Toss lightly together with dressing made of:

½ cup tarragon wine vinegar
½ cup chili sauce
¼ cup safflower oil
Sea salt, to taste

Serve on lettuce and sprinkle with toasted sesame or sunflower seeds.
Serves 6

Seafood Salads

Shrimp Salad

3 cups cooked large shrimp
1 cup chopped celery
6 small potatoes cooked in jackets and diced
½ cucumber, sliced thin with peel
1 cup sprouts
2 hard-boiled eggs, chopped

Combine ingredients and mix with a dressing of:

½ cup mayonnaise
½ cup yogurt
1 teaspoon kelp granules

Heap on a platter lined with lettuce leaves. Sprinkle with ¼ cup almond slivers browned in butter and garnish with clumps of sprouts.
Serves 3–4

Avocado and Crab Salad

2 avocados
Lemon juice
1 pound cooked crab meat
½ cup mayonnaise
¾ cup whipped cream
1 tablespoon minced onion
2 tablespoons chili sauce
½ teaspoon sea salt
Freshly ground pepper
Toasted sesame seeds

Cut avocado in half carefully to reserve shells. Cut down to pit and gently twist avocado so that it separates into halves. Remove pit and carefully cut out avocado segments without piercing peel. Dice avocados, sprinkle with lemon juice, and brush inside of shells with lemon juice to keep them from discoloring. Blend crab meat with mayonnaise, whipped cream, minced onion, chili sauce, salt, and pepper. Combine crab meat mixture with diced avocado and fill shells. Add more mayonnaise or lemon juice if needed. Sprinkle with toasted sesame seeds.
Serves 4

Sole Salad

4 filets of sole
4 limes
Lettuce
Unrefined olive oil
Kelp
Sea salt
Lime slices

Marinate sole in juice of limes for 1 hour or more. Sauté lightly on both sides in butter. Chill and serve on lettuce. Sprinkle sole with a little oil, kelp, and salt. Garnish with lime slices.
Serves 4

Olives and Celery

Tuna and Olive Salad

1 bunch lettuce, torn-up
1 tomato, peeled, seeded, and cut in eighths
6 green olives, pitted and quartered
6 black olives, pitted and quartered
¼ cup diced celery
½ cup flaked tuna

Combine above ingredients and toss lightly with each of the following (separately):

3 tablespoons unrefined olive oil
1 tablespoon lemon juice

Shake sea salt, kelp, and pepper over salad and toss well again.
Serves 4–6

Sardine Salad

4 boiled potatoes, diced
2 small beets, diced
2 cans skinless, boneless sardines, drained and mashed
1 tablespoon chopped onion
1 garlic clove, minced

Combine above ingredients.

½ cup mayonnaise, thinned with lemon juice
¼ teaspoon ginger
½ teaspoon marjoram

Mix mayonnaise, ginger, and marjoram and toss with sardine-vegetable mixture. Serve on lettuce.
Serves 6

Shrimp and Avocado Salad

1 pound small, boiled shrimp
2 tablespoons lime juice
¼ cup safflower oil
1 green onion, chopped fine
1 tablespoon chili sauce
¼ teaspoon sea salt
3 ripe avocados

Combine lime juice, oil, onion, chili sauce, and salt. Marinate shrimp in this mixture for 1 hour or more in refrigerator. Cut 3 ripe avocados in half, remove pit, and heap each half with shrimp mixture. Sprinkle with paprika and kelp granules and serve on lettuce.
Serves 6

Salad Dressings

The simplest salad dressing is basic French or Italian dressing. Be sure lettuce leaves are dry so that oil will adhere to the leaves. When salad greens and other ingredients are assembled and ready to be dressed, first pour oil over them, 1 tablespoon per serving, and toss well. Then put 1 teaspoon lemon juice, cider vinegar, or wine vinegar per serving over salad and toss again. Sprinkle with sea salt and pepper and toss lightly again. Each leaf should then be shiny and well seasoned. Other ingredients may be added and tossed in with salt and pepper, such as, herbs, kelp powder, seeds, and nuts (ground, chopped, or whole), Worcestershire sauce, and raw egg. A salad bowl may first be rubbed with a split garlic clove before putting salad ingredients into it; this adds immeasureably to the salad (even for those who don't as a rule care for garlic).

Salad Dressings [Combinations]

Make in jars and keep refrigerated. Shake or stir well each time before using.

Curry Mayonnaise

★ 1 cup mayonnaise, 1 teaspoon curry powder (more if desired), and 1 tablespoon tamari soy sauce.

Celery Seed Dressing

★ ½ cup unrefined olive or safflower oil, ½ cup wine vinegar, 4 shallots (or green onions) minced, 1 teaspoon dry mustard, 2 teaspoons celery seeds, 1 teaspoon sea salt, 1 teaspoon lemon juice, ¼ teaspoon pepper, and 1 teaspoon honey.

Basil Dressing

★ ½ cup unrefined olive oil or sesame oil, 2 tablespoons lemon juice, 1 garlic clove split and left in jar, 1 tablespoon onion minced, ¼ teaspoon thyme, 1 teaspoon basil, ¼ teaspoon pepper, and ½ teaspoon sea salt.

Yogurt Dressing

★ ¾ cup yogurt, 1 tablespoon cider vinegar, 1 teaspoon honey, 1 teaspoon sea salt, ½ teaspoon kelp powder, ¼ teaspoon coarsely ground pepper, 1 garlic clove crushed, and 1 teaspoon poppy or caraway seeds (optional).

Mint Dressing

★ 6 tablespoons unrefined olive oil or safflower oil, 2 tablespoons cider vinegar, 2 tablespoons chopped parsley, 2 tablespoons chopped mint (1 tablespoon dried mint), ¼ teaspoon sea salt, and freshly ground pepper.

Thousand Island Dressing

★ 1 cup mayonnaise, ¼ cup chili sauce, 4 stuffed olives chopped, 1 tablespoon chopped chives, and ½ teaspoon paprika.

Dill Dressing

★ 1 cup yogurt (or ½ cup yogurt mixed with ½ cup mayonnaise), 2 tablespoons lemon juice, ¼ teaspoon sea salt, ¼ teaspoon kelp powder, ⅛ teaspoon pepper, a garlic clove crushed, 1 teaspoon dill, and ½ teaspoon paprika.

Curry Vinegrette

★ Rub the yolks of 3 hard-boiled eggs into ½ cup safflower oil; stir in 2 tablespoons cider vinegar, 1 teaspoon curry powder, ¼ teaspoon sea salt, and dash of pepper.

Tamari Dressing

★ ½ cup safflower oil, ¼ cup cider vinegar, 2 teaspoons tamari soy sauce, 1 teaspoon basil, 1 teaspoon honey, and ½ teaspoon sea salt.

Herb Dressing

★ ¼ cup unrefined olive oil or all-blend oil, 1 tablespoon wine vinegar, 1 teaspoon minced onion, ½ garlic clove minced, ¼ teaspoon each thyme, basil, and marjoram, ½ teaspoon chopped parsley, ½ teaspoon sea salt, a dash freshly ground pepper, and 1 teaspoon sesame or sunflower seeds.

Fruit Salad Dressing

★ ½ cup mayonnaise mixed with ½ to 1 cup whipped cream, ¼ teaspoon nutmeg, and 1 teaspoon honey.

Mayonnaise

2 egg yolks
1 tablespoon lemon juice
¾ teaspoon sea salt
1 cup safflower oil

Use an electric blender.

Both egg yolks and oil should be at room temperature.

Put the egg yolks in the blender with the lemon juice, salt, and ¼ cup of the oil.

Blend a few seconds until the yolks and oil have emulsified. Add the remaining oil in a thin stream. The very last bit of oil may not blend through; simply stir it through with your spatula as you pour the mayonnaise into a jar. For thicker mayonnaise, blend longer. For fluffy mayonnaise, use 1 egg yolk and 1 whole egg.

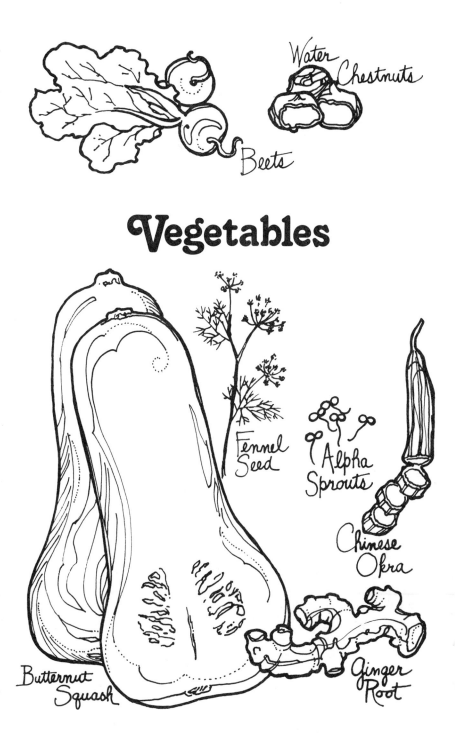

Water Chestnuts

Beets

Vegetables

Fennel Seed

Alpha Sprouts

Chinese Okra

Butternut Squash

Ginger Root

There are simple but strict rules to observe in preparing vegetables if the results are to be nutritious, colorful, and altogether enticing. While the finest cuisines in the world feature vegetables and treat them with love and tenderness, we in America often ruin them with overcooking. We can, however, easily master the art of preparing vegetables. This is important because surveys show that the average American diet is lacking in fresh vegetables. This means our diets are lacking in the essential nutrients vegetables provide.

Vegetables must be fresh. The least amount of time that elapses between the garden and the palate the better. The younger vegetables are, the sweeter and more tender they are; and, generally speaking, the deeper in color vegetables are, the more flavor and food value they contain.

Produce from organic farmers, home gardens, or home hothouse gardens (now available to homeownerrs) is the most ideal, and we should make every effort to avail ourselves of such. The Rodale Press of Emmaus, Pennsylvania, publishes a book entitled *The Organic Directory*, which gives information on organic produce, suppliers, and co-ops. Advice on organic gardening may also be obtained from the Rodale Press, who publish the magazine *Organic Gardening and Farming*, and who also have classes on organic gardening. For listings on these classes, send a self-addressed envelope to Organic Classroom, *Organic Gardening and Farming Magazine*, Emmaus, Pennsylvania 18049. There are other excellent books on organic gardening available through bookstores and natural food stores.

One form of gardening we can easily do in our own kitchens is to grow sprouts. The most powerful part of the plant is the seed; it produces life and, therefore, contains the life-giving elements. Seeds are packed with the vitamins, minerals, and other plant food elements we know about and all those that are not yet discovered. And they may be included in our daily diet in many delicious ways as demonstrated in the recipes in this book.

Sprouted seeds are extremely healthful, and there is no trick at all to growing them. I have two or three on hand in my refrigerator at all times to add to cooked vegetables, salads, and sandwiches. Buy untreated seeds at your natural food store—I suggest that you start with mung bean, alfalfa, and/or red clover seeds. Put 2 tablespoons of each in a wide-mouth jar and pour *spring* water over them. Make a top of nylon netting secured with a rubber band. I use two thicknesses of netting, placing them at opposite angles to make smaller holes so that tiny seeds do not go through. Soak the seeds a few hours and drain well by turning the jar upside down. Place the jar in a dark place or cover with a brown paper bag to keep out the light. Every morning and evening when you go into the kitchen to prepare a meal, pour a little spring water over the seeds, drain well, and return it to the dark spot. Do this each morning for three days, and you will have beautiful sprouts. They should only be from one-half to one inch long. Place alfalfa or red clover sprouts in the sunshine for a few hours to take on a little green, nature's chlorophyll. Screw the lid onto the jar and place in the refrigerator.

Many seeds may be successfully grown at home, and they vary in both time and extent of growth. For instance, soybeans and peas take five days. Most natural food stores carry seeds and a variety of sprouters with instructions.

When preparing vegetables, wash quickly in cold water and either cook immediately or dry immediately and chill at once to retain as much vitamin and mineral value as possible. Vegetables should never be soaked.

Vegetables should be peeled, sliced, and chopped just before eating or cooking, but do not peel them if you know they have not been sprayed with insecticides; there is nutrition in the peel and the layer just under the peel. Except for grains, vegetables are most nutritious eaten raw, but they retain an appreciable amount of their food value if cooked briefly. There are three great mistakes Americans make in cooking vegetables: first, they cook in too much water; second, they overcook the vegetable; and, third, they pour the water, which has extracted valuable nutrients from the vegetable, down the drain.

The best methods for cooking tender vegetables are stir-frying in Chinese fashion or steaming over a little boiling water. Many stores carry stainless steel steaming racks that will fit into ordinary pans with lids. If vegetables are to be cooked in water, use as little water as possible, cook only until the vegetables are tender, and save the water to use in soups and sauces.

Do not reheat vegetables; use them chilled in salads. By all means eat a wide variety of vegetables regularly. This is easily accomplished because in our country we have a vast choice of vegetables year-round, we have many interesting seasonings to lend variety to vegetable dishes, and the nutritional methods of preparation are simple.

Stir-Fry

Use a heavy skillet or wok (Chinese pot) over medium heat and pour in enough oil to cover the bottom. Use a wooden spoon to stir vegetables because it is gentler on them.

Wash and cut up vegetables. A vegetable may be cooked by itself or combined with other vegetables.

If using onions or celery, cook them briefly first, then add other vegetables according to their tenderness. In other words, put in the vegetables which require more cooking first, and those which require least cooking last. Stir vegetables gently while cooking. If sprouts are to be included, combine them at the very end of the cooking time, just long enough to warm the sprouts. The overall cooking time of tender vegetables is 3 to 5 minutes. For less-tender vegetables, put lid on pan for a few more minutes. Vegetables cooked in this manner stay crisp and bright in color.

Steaming

Place a wire steaming rack over about an inch of boiling water. Use a pan with a lid. Steam vegetables long enough to become tender but still crisp, approximately 4 to 6 minutes.

Seasonings

Among the twists which add flavor, color, texture, and interest to vegetable dishes are:

Minced garlic
Minced onions or shallots
Tamari soy sauce
Vegetable seasoning powders
Kelp powder
Chopped walnuts or pecans
Slivered almonds browned in butter
Sesame, sunflower, pumpkin, celery, or caraway seeds
Olives, green or ripe
Whole-grain croutons
Chopped mint, fresh or dried
Chopped parsley, fresh or dried
Herbs, such as thyme, marjoram, basil, rosemary, etc.

Some attractive combinations of vegetables are:
★ Cauliflower sections, broccoli tips and broccoli stems sliced, carrots in thin strips with minced garlic.
★ Cut green beans and wax beans and tomatoes, seeded and cut in eighths, with sunflower seeds.
★ Chopped onions, sliced zucchini, and small yellow squash, with oregano.
★ Sautéed artichoke hearts dipped lightly in whole wheat flour and sesame seeds.
★ Celery, peas, mushrooms, sprouts, and a little marjoram.
★ Bean sprouts, bamboo shoots, water chestnuts, mushrooms, spinach leaves, and tamari soy sauce.
★ Red cabbage, white cabbage, green pepper, and apple slices, with celery or caraway seeds.
★ Sliced sweet onion, celery, jicama root, carrots, and green pepper.
★ Spinach leaves with whole pecans, seasoned with vegetable salt, kelp powder, or grated nutmeg.

Soybean Casserole

1½ cups dried soybeans
½ onion, cut up
½ teaspoon thyme
1 cup chopped celery
½ cup chopped green pepper
2 tomatoes, peeled and chopped
3 tablespoons minced parsley
2 garlic cloves, crushed
½ teaspoon sea salt
3 tablespoons nutritional yeast
3 tablespoons soy flour
½ cup chopped nuts

Place soybeans in a heavy pan. Pour boiling water over to cover beans. Add onion and thyme and simmer for 2 minutes. Remove from heat and soak for 1 hour. Simmer 2½ hours, or until tender, and drain.

Preheat oven to 350°.

Combine soybeans with remaining ingredients and turn into an oiled casserole. Bake at 350° for 30 minutes.
Serves 6

Curried Soybeans

1½ cups dried soybeans
½ onion, cut up
¾ cup yogurt
2 tablespoons curry powder (more or less
    according to taste)
¼ cup raisins

Place soybeans in a heavy pan. Pour boiling water over to cover beans and simmer for 2 minutes. Remove from heat and soak 1 hour. Add onion, and simmer for 2½ to 3 hours, or until tender, and drain.

Combine curry powder with yogurt and stir into beans. Add raisins and heat through. Do not boil.
Serves 6

Tomatoes

Green Beans and Tomatoes

12 pounds green beans
6 onions, sliced
4 pounds tomatoes, chopped
1 tablespoon marjoram
¼ pound butter

Wash beans and leave whole. Simmer until tender in just enough boiling water to cover. Add tomatoes and simmer 3 minutes longer. Drain and toss with butter and marjoram.
Serves 50

Green Beans and Cheese Casserole

4 eggs
½ teaspoon kelp powder
1 teaspoon sea salt
2 tablespoons minced onion
2 cups grated Swiss cheese
½ cup cottage cheese
2 pounds green beans, sliced
Wheat germ

Preheat oven to 350°.

Beat eggs, then beat in kelp, salt, onion, and cheeses.

Spread half of the green beans in the bottom of a buttered 2-quart baking dish and pour half of the egg mixture over them.

Spread the remaining beans over the mixture and top with remaining egg mixture. Sprinkle with wheat germ and bake at 350° for 30 to 40 minutes or until set and lightly browned.
Serves 6–8

Lentils

Green Beans With Almonds

¼ cup slivered almonds
Butter
2 pounds green beans
1 cup sprouts

Brown almond slivers in a little butter and set aside.

Cut green beans and steam for 5 or 6 minutes, just until tender. Add sprouts at the last minute to warm through.

Toss beans, sprouts, and almonds together and serve.
Serves 6–8

Lima Bean Loaf

2 cups cooked lima beans
½ cup wheat germ
½ cup whole-wheat bread crumbs
1 tablespoon nutritional yeast
½ cup onions, chopped fine
½ cup chopped walnuts
½ teaspoon sea salt
2 eggs, well-beaten
½ cup cream
½ cup butter

Preheat oven to 350°.

Combine lima beans, wheat germ, bread crumbs, yeast, onions, nuts, salt, eggs, cream, and 2 tablespoons butter.

Turn into a 9″x5″ loaf pan and bake at 350° for 45 minutes, basting with remaining butter several times during baking period.
Serves 6

Lima Beans Smetane

2 cups or packages frozen lima beans
2 tablespoons butter
½ onion, sliced thin
1 tablespoon arrowroot
½ teaspoon sea salt
1 teaspoon paprika
½ cup sour cream

Cook the beans in ½ cup boiling water until tender. Drain, reserving liquid.

Sauté onion in butter until transparent. Stir in liquid, arrowroot, salt, and paprika. Blend well and simmer until slightly thickened.

Add sour cream over low heat and add the beans, stirring. Heat through but do not boil
Serves 6

Lentils With Barley

½ medium onion, chopped
1 garlic clove, crushed
½ cup chopped celery
Butter
3 tomatoes, peeled and chopped
2 cups chicken broth or water
½ cup dried lentils
½ cup barley
½ teaspoon sea salt
¼ teaspoon sage
¼ teaspoon rosemary

In a heavy saucepan sauté the onion and garlic in a little butter until onion is transparent. Add the celery and cook, stirring, 3 minutes.

Add remaining ingredients and simmer 30 to 45 minutes or until lentils and barley are tender.
Serves 4

mushrooms

Barley and Mushroom Casserole

½ pound mushrooms, sliced
3 tablespoons butter
2 medium onions, coarsely chopped
¼ pound butter
1½ cups barley
4 cups chicken stock (or bouillon)
½ teaspoon sea salt

Cook mushrooms in 3 tablespoons butter for 1 minute. Set aside.

Sauté onions in ¼ pound butter until they are wilted, then add the barley.

Stir over heat until barley gets beautifully browned—*this is important.* Put in casserole or electric skillet; add mushrooms and chicken stock.

Cover and cook over medium heat or in a 350° oven for 30 minutes, adding salt and more stock if mixture seems too dry.

The dish is ready when the barley is tender but not mushy.
Serves 6

Beets With Orange

6 medium beets
¾ cup orange juice
2 teaspoons lemon juice
4 tablespoons butter
1 teaspoon sea salt
1 teaspoon dried mint
1 tablespoon arrowroot

Peel and grate beets.

Combine ½ cup orange juice, lemon juice, butter, and salt in a saucepan and bring to a boil; add beets, cover, and simmer for 10 minutes.

Mix the remaining ¼ cup orange juice with the mint and arrowroot and stir into beets. Simmer, stirring, until clear and thickened.
Serves 6

Russian Beets

2 pounds beets, cooked and cubed
Honey
1 teaspoon dried tarragon
2 tablespoons butter
Tarragon vinegar

Drizzle a bit of honey over hot beet cubes, sprinkle with dried tarragon, add butter, and toss gently.

Serve with tarragon vinegar on the side.
Serves 6

Polish Beets

6 medium beets, cooked
2 tablespoons butter
1 tablespoon whole-wheat flour
1 cup milk, warmed
½ teaspoon vegetable salt
1 tablespoon lemon juice

Peel and grate beets.

Melt butter, add flour, and simmer 3 minutes. Stir in warm milk and simmer 3 more minutes. Add vegetable salt and lemon juice and pour over beets. Heat through and serve.
Serves 4–6

French Broccoli

1 large bunch broccoli
3 tablespoons melted butter
1 tablespoon lemon juice
Chopped chives
¼ cup slivered almonds, browned in butter

Wash broccoli; remove the coarse leaves and slice lower stalks. Place on steamer rack over hot water and steam 6 minutes, just until tender.

Remove broccoli to a warm serving plate; pour over it the melted butter mixed with lemon juice, sprinkle with chives and browned almond slivers
Serves 4–6

Broccoli

Stir-Fry Broccoli

1 large bunch broccoli
¼ cup unrefined olive oil or safflower oil
2 cloves garlic, crushed
2 tablespoons chopped, stuffed olives (optional)
Sesame seeds

Wash broccoli; remove the coarse leaves, slice lower stalks, and separate flowerets.

Heat olive oil in a heavy skillet, or wok, and add garlic. Cook 1 minute. Add broccoli and stir-fry 5 minutes. Add olives, if used, place cover over pan, and steam just until broccoli is tender.

Cook sesame seeds in a small, dry skillet until browned.

Place broccoli in a warm serving dish, sprinkle with sesame seeds, and serve.
Serves 4–6

Brussels Sprouts in Casserole

2 pounds Brussels sprouts
4 tablespoons butter
2 tablespoons chopped onions
¼ pound mushrooms, sliced
1 tablespoon lemon juice
Warm milk
Whole-wheat bread crumbs
Butter

Preheat oven to 350°.

Wash sprouts well and trim.

Sauté onions and mushrooms in butter until onions are transparent and toss with sprouts and lemon juice.

Turn into a casserole dish, pour over mixture enough milk to cover. Sprinkle with bread crumbs and dot with butter.

Bake at 350° for 15 minutes or until Brussels sprouts are tender but still firm. If crumbs are not brown, place under broiler until lightly browned.
Serves 6–8

Note: Whole-wheat bread crumbs may be mixed, half and half, with wheat germ or grated Parmesan cheese.

Austrian Cabbage

1 head red cabbage
Oil
½ cup white wine or apple juice
1 teaspoon honey
2 apples, sliced with peel on
6 chestnuts, parboiled and cut up, or
    ¼ cup cashews (optional)

Wash and shred cabbage. Cook it in a little oil a few minutes.

Add wine, honey, apple slices, and nuts, if used, and cook gently until everything is tender.
Serves 6

Mung Beans & Sprouts

Cabbage Casserole

2 pounds cabbage
5 tablespoons butter
5 tablespoons brown rice flour
2 cups cabbage water
1 tablespoon dill seed
1 tablespoon sherry or tamari soy sauce
1 teaspoon sea salt
½ cup mung bean sprouts
2 tablespoons wheat germ

Shred cabbage and cook in a little water for 5 minutes. Drain, reserving ½ cup.

In a heavy saucepan melt butter, add flour, and simmer 3 minutes; add cabbage water and simmer, stirring for 3 more minutes. Add cabbage, dill seed, sherry or tamari, salt, and sprouts, mixing well.

Turn cabbage mixture into a casserole, sprinkle with wheat germ, and brown under broiler.
Serves 6

Swedish Cauliflower

3 pounds cauliflower
3 tablespoons butter
1 tablespoon lemon juice
¼ cup whole-wheat bread crumbs
¼ cup wheat germ
3 hard-boiled eggs, chopped
1 teaspoon parsley flakes
¼ teaspoon sea salt
Nutmeg

Wash cauliflower and place on steamer rack over hot water, cover, and steam 6 minutes, or just until tender. Remove to warm platter and keep warm.

Melt butter with lemon juice and add bread crumbs and wheat germ; cook until browned. Pour over cauliflower and sprinkle with chopped eggs, parsley, salt and nutmeg.
Serves 6

Polish Cauliflower

1 head cauliflower
3 tablespoons butter
3 tablespoons brown rice flour
2 cups warm milk
¼ teaspoon sea salt
1 tablespoon grated Parmesan cheese
¼ teaspoon nutmeg
2 eggs, beaten

Preheat oven to 350°.

Wash cauliflower and separate the flowerets.

Melt butter, stir in flour, and simmer 3 minutes. Stir in warm milk and simmer 3 more minutes. Add salt, cheese, nutmeg, and eggs.

Combine sauce with cauliflowerets and turn into a buttered casserole. Bake at 350° for 30 minutes.
Serves 6

Eggplant

Baked Eggplant

2 onions, large
1 medium eggplant
6 tomatoes
½ cup unrefined olive oil
Garlic powder
Sea salt
Paprika
Basil
Oregano
¼ cup grated Parmesan cheese
¼ cup cream
Wheat germ

Preheat oven to 325°.

Slice onions, then slice eggplant and tomatoes ¼-inch thick with skins on.

Pour oil into a baking dish and place layers of onions, eggplant, and tomatoes alternately, sprinkling with garlic, salt, paprika, basil, and oregano. Repeat until vegetables are used up.

Bake, covered, at 325° for 50 minutes.

Combine Parmesan cheese and cream and pour over the top of the vegetables. Sprinkle with wheat germ and bake uncovered at 400° for 10 minutes longer or until lightly browned.
Serves 6

Leeks

Eggplant With Mushrooms and Cheese

2 eggplants
Brown rice flour
Oil
6 mushrooms, sliced
2 small onions, sliced
Butter
3 tablespoons butter
3 tablespoons brown rice flour
¼ cup grated Gruyère and Parmesan cheeses, mixed
¾ cup milk
Sea salt and pepper
1 teaspoon dry mustard
Wheat germ

Cut eggplants in half, dust the tops lightly with flour, and put top downward in hot oil in a heavy pan, cover and cook slowly for 10 minutes.

Sauté mushrooms and onions in a little butter until onions are transparent but not brown. Add 3 tablespoons butter and, when melted, add the flour, stirring. Add the cheese, milk, salt, pepper, and mustard and simmer 3 minutes.

Scoop out the meat from the eggplants and chop coarsely. Combine with the mushroom-cheese sauce and fill the eggplant skins.

Dot with butter, sprinkle with wheat germ, and brown under the broiler.
Serves 4

Eggplant Casserole

8 to 10 pounds eggplant
1 quart chicken broth
2 cups sour cream
1 teaspoon sea salt
1 tablespoon paprika
½ cup butter melted with ½ cup safflower oil
4 cups whole-wheat bread crumbs
1 tablespoon basil

Preheat oven to 350°.

Wash and slice eggplant ¼-inch thick with peel on. Simmer in a little water for 5 minutes or just until tender.

Lay eggplant slices in oiled baking dishes.

Combine chicken broth, sour cream, salt, paprika, and butter with safflower oil and pour over eggplant slices. Shake the pans to distribute sauce.

Combine bread crumbs with basil and sprinkle over eggplant. Bake at 350° for 30 minutes.
Serves 50

Minted Peas and Carrots

4 pounds carrots, diced
5 pounds peas
Boiling water
1 tablespoon sea salt
¼ cup chopped mint or mint flakes
8 ounces butter

In covered pan, cook carrots and peas in minimum amount boiling water for about 5 minutes or until vegetables are tender.

Drain slightly but keep a little of the liquid with the vegetables; the liquid not only contains important vitamins and minerals, but helps keep the vegetables warm while serving.

Stir in salt, mint flakes, and butter and serve.
Serves 25

French Green Peas

4 pounds peas
1 head lettuce
1 tablespoon cornstarch
1 tablespoon water
1 cup canned pearl onions
¼ teaspoon thyme
¼ teaspoon tarragon
¼ teaspoon sea salt
Freshly ground pepper
Chopped chives

Cut the lettuce into eighths and cook with the peas in 1 cup water a few minutes, just until tender.

Mix cornstarch with water and stir into vegetables; simmer until slightly thickened.

Add onions, thyme, tarragon, sea salt, and a few grindings of pepper. Heat through, turn into warm serving dish, and sprinkle with chives.
Serves 8

Green Peas With Ginger

4 pounds peas
¼ cup tamari soy sauce
1 tablespoon cornstarch
¼ teaspoon ginger powder

In a skillet or wok cook peas in tamari 4 minutes. Add more tamari if needed.

Dissolve cornstarch in 1 tablespoon water and add to the peas; cook, stirring, until thickened.

Stir in ginger powder and serve.
Serves 6

Green Pea Purée

4 pounds peas
½ teaspoon sea salt
¼ teaspoon nutmeg
½ teaspoon dried mint (optional)
2 tablespoons butter

Cook peas in a little water for 3 minutes.

Pour the peas with the water in which they were cooked into a blender. Blend 1 minute and add salt, nutmeg, mint, and butter. Blend a second longer and serve.
Serves 6

Italian Stuffed Potatoes

6 baking potatoes
6 tablespoons warm milk
6 tablespoons butter
1 egg yolk
1 garlic clove, crushed
Sea salt and pepper
Grated Parmesan cheese

Bake the potatoes after rubbing them with a little oil to keep them soft.

Cut off the tops and scoop out the pulp. Beat pulp with milk, butter, egg yolk, garlic, and a little salt and pepper.

Stuff the pulp back into the skins, sprinkle with Parmesan cheese, and brown under the broiler.
Serves 6

Potatoes

French Potatoes

3 potatoes
3 onions
Butter
Gruyère, Parmesan, or cottage cheese
Sea salt and pepper
½ cup chicken broth
Wheat germ

Preheat oven to 350°.

Scrub potatoes, peel onions, and slice into thin slices.

Butter a baking dish and arrange the potato and onion slices with cheese and seasonings in alternate layers.

Pour the chicken broth over all and sprinkle wheat germ over the top. Dot with butter and bake at 350° for 1 hour or until potatoes are tender.
Serves 6

Polish Potatoes

5 potatoes
Butter
1 onion, chopped
Sea salt and pepper
Whole-wheat bread crumbs
Dry cottage cheese
2 eggs, slightly beaten
1 cup sour cream

Preheat oven to 400°.

Cook the potatoes in their jackets until tender. Slice and lay in a buttered baking dish.

Sauté the onion lightly in butter and add to the potatoes. Sprinkle a little salt, pepper, and bread crumbs over the potatoes and then spread cottage cheese on top.

Beat the eggs into the sour cream and pour over potatoes. Bake at 400° until bubbly and browned.
Serves 6

Ginger Root

East Indian Potatoes

3 large potatoes
¼ cup yogurt
1 tablespoon curry powder
3 tablespoons oil
½ teaspoon sea salt
1 teaspoon powdered ginger

Boil the potatoes in their jackets. Drain, peel, and cut into cubes.

Mix the yogurt and curry powder and toss with the potato cubes.

Heat the oil in a skillet with the salt and ginger.

Brown the potatoes in oil and serve.
Serves 6

Sweet Potato Pudding

16 pounds sweet potatoes
2 quarts milk
1 cup butter
1 tablespoon nutmeg
4 cups crushed unsweetened pineapple
Wheat germ

Preheat oven to 350°.

Boil potatoes in their jackets until tender. Drain, scoop out pulp, and mash.

Heat milk with butter, add to the potatoes, and mash well together. Stir in nutmeg and pineapple.

Turn into buttered baking pans, sprinkle with wheat germ and bake at 350° for 40 minutes.
Serves 50

Brown Rice

1 cup brown rice
2½ cups water
¼ teaspoon sea salt

Put all ingredients into a saucepan and bring to a boil.

Cover and simmer about 35 minutes or until water is absorbed and the rice is separate and tender.

If rice is still moist, cook uncovered until dry. (Rice may be cooked uncovered for entire cooking period by using 3 cups water to 1 cup rice and ¼ teaspoon sea salt.)
Serves 4–6

Rice With Almonds Iraq

1 cup brown rice
2½ cups chicken broth or water
¼ teaspoon sea salt
2 pounds peas
Butter
1 cup slivered almonds
Cinnamon
Nutmeg
Fresh mint, chopped (or dried mint flakes)

Put rice, broth or water, and salt into a saucepan and bring to a boil. Cover and simmer 35 minutes or until liquid is absorbed.

Cook peas in a little water for 5 minutes or until tender.

Brown almond slivers in butter.

Combine rice, peas, and almonds. Sprinkle with cinnamon, nutmeg, and mint. Toss lightly and serve.
Serves 6

West Indian Rice

2 cups shredded coconut
3 cups milk
1 onion, chopped
Oil
Sea salt
1½ cups brown rice
1 teaspoon cinnamon

Soak the coconut in the milk for 1 hour, then simmer for 10 minutes. Squeeze out the coconut, reserving milk.

In a large saucepan, brown onion lightly in oil and add the coconut, milk, salt, and rice. Bring to a boil, cover and simmer for about 35 minutes or until liquid is absorbed.

Turn into a warm serving dish, sprinkle with cinnamon, and serve.
Serves 6

Casserole Verte

3 pounds spinach
3 eggs
¾ cup half milk and half cream
3 tablespoons butter, melted
½ teaspoon sea salt

Preheat oven to 400°.

Wash spinach and place in saucepan with water remaining on leaves. Cover and cook only until leaves are wilted.

Put in blender with liquid from pan and purée.

Add eggs, cream and milk, butter, and salt and blend a minute.

Pour into buttered baking dish and set in pan of hot water. Bake at 400° for 50 minutes to 1 hour or until firm. It will be very light and bright green in color.
Serves 6

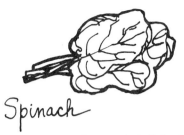

Spinach

Spinach With Olives

Unrefined olive oil
2 garlic cloves, minced
1 tablespoon slivered almonds
3 pounds spinach, washed
¼ cup green olives, sliced
¼ cup ripe olives, sliced
½ teaspoon nutmeg

Over medium heat, heat enough oil to cover bottom of skillet; stir in the garlic and nuts and cook until lightly browned.

Add spinach, olives, and nutmeg. Toss and cook only until spinach has wilted.
Serves 4–6

Spinach and Mushrooms

12 large mushrooms
Tamari soy sauce
4 pounds spinach, washed
¼ cup sesame seeds

Clean and slice mushrooms and sauté in a little tamari; set aside.

Brown sesame seeds in a dry skillet and set aside.

Cook spinach in the water that clings to the leaves after washing; cook only until wilted.

Combine mushrooms, spinach, and sesame seeds and serve.
Serves 6

Tip: Brown a quantity of sesame seeds and store what you are not using in a covered jar for future use.

Italian Spinach

4 pounds fresh spinach
½ cup butter
Sea salt
Pepper
Pinch of nutmeg
¼ cup grated Parmesan or Romano cheese

Wash spinach well and cook in the butter until just tender.

Add a little salt and pepper, the nutmeg, and the cheese. Mix thoroughly over heat and serve immediately.

Serves 6

Stuffed Zucchini

4 medium zucchini
¼ cup unrefined olive oil, or sesame oil
½ cup chopped onion
1 clove garlic, minced
2 medium tomatoes, peeled and chopped
½ cup wheat germ
2 tablespoons minced parsley
½ teaspoon sea salt
¼ teaspoon freshly ground pepper
½ teaspoon oregano
Unrefined olive oil, or sesame oil

Preheat oven to 350°.

Scrub zucchini and cook whole in a little water for 3 minutes. Drain and cut in half lengthwise; scoop out pulp and chop.

Heat oil and sauté onion lightly, add zucchini pulp and garlic, cook 3 minutes. Mix in tomatoes and cook 2 minutes longer.

Stuff the shells and place on an oiled baking sheet.

Mix wheat germ with herbs and seasonings and sprinkle over zucchini. Dot with oil and bake at 350° for 20 minutes.

Serves 4–8

Grecian Squash

4 small yellow crookneck squash
1 garlic clove, crushed
Unrefined olive oil
¼ teaspoon sea salt
1 teaspoon honey
1 teaspoon chopped mint
3 tablespoons cider vinegar

Wash squash and slice thin. Sauté with garlic in oil until tender.

Add the salt, honey, mint, and vinegar and cook 3 minutes longer.
Serves 4–6

Acorn Squash

1 acorn squash
Butter
Sea salt
Kelp powder
Honey

Preheat oven to 350°.

Scrub squash, cut in half, and scoop out seeds.

Put a little butter, salt, kelp, and honey in each cavity. Place squash halves in a baking pan with about an inch of hot water in it.

Bake at 350° for 40 minutes or until tender, depending on size of the squash.
Serves 2

Acorn Squash

Broiled Tomatoes

4 large, firm tomatoes
1½ teaspoons vegetable salt
4 tablespoons minced onion
2 tablespoons minced parsley or parsley flakes
Wheat germ
Butter

Wash tomatoes, cut out the core at stem end, then cut tomatoes in half crosswise.

Sprinkle with salt, onion, parsley, and wheat germ. Dot with butter and broil about 10 minutes or until tender and browned.
Serves 4–8

Baked Tomatoes and Corn

4 tomatoes, peeled and chopped
3 cups corn kernels cut off cobs
2 green onions, chopped fine
¼ teaspoon sea salt
¼ teaspoon kelp powder
2 eggs, yolks and whites beaten separately
2 tablespoons whole-wheat bread crumbs
2 tablespoons grated Parmesan cheese

Preheat oven to 375°.

Combine tomatoes, corn, onions, salt, kelp, and beaten egg yolks.

Beat egg whites stiff but not dry and fold into vegetable mixture; pour into a buttered baking dish.

Combine bread crumbs with cheese and sprinkle over vegetable mixture. Bake at 375° for 40 minutes.
Serves 6

Quince

Swiss Cheese

Desserts

Pineapple

Mint Leaves

Pie

Pumpkin Seeds

Watermelon

Carob Powder

Kiwi Fruit

Strawberries

Figs

Desserts have probably brought our nation more ill health than any other part of the standard American diet. For instance, apple pie à la mode is not only made from "enriched" flour, which contains only a fraction of the vitamins and minerals that are important to good health, but numerous chemical additives are found in both the flour and the ice cream. Besides these drawbacks, piecrust is usually made from hydrogenated fat and one slice of pie à la mode contains a minimum of one-quarter cup of sugar!

We need to make a drastic change in our desserts if we are to be healthy and promote the healthful growth of our children. Such a change does not mean eliminating pies, cakes, cookies, puddings, and ice cream; it means making them of healthful ingredients. A word of caution, however: Desserts should not be too sweet. Although such sweeteners as honey and molasses are vastly preferable to sugar, they should be used with restraint. Our constitutions were not designed to metabolize large portions of concentrated sweets in any form. We should use as little sweetening as possible and none at all in many cases. It is wise to use even less sweetening than called for in following recipes, and such a step will follow quite naturally as palates become reeducated to healthful foods. It is a fact that when we have not had sugar for a while, we no longer crave it and overly sweetened foods become distasteful to us.

Taste is a matter of habit; it can be changed in a surprisingly short period of time. And, crucially, a taste for healthful foods—not oversweetened, overly salted food—should be fostered in children from the cradle up.

Healthful dessert habits mean eating sweetened desserts only occasionally and eating cookies neither by the handful nor regularly. The most healthful dessert is beautiful fresh fruit and cheese, which is the usual fare of many nations and of healthy people.

Fruit

All cut-up fresh fruits in season or unsweetened frozen fruits are delicious and colorful when combined, such as: apples sliced or cubed with peels left on; orange, grapefruit, tangerine, and tangelo sections; all berries; seedless or seeded grapes; sliced bananas; kiwis (with seeds left in); papayas; avocados; jicamas; mangoes; pears; peaches; apricots; coconut; pineapple; and all varieties of melons.

Suggestions for serving fruit attractively:

Melon Halves

Cantaloupe, honeydew, etc., and watermelon for a large group. Scoop out melons, reserving pulp. Fill with:

Strawberries
Pineapple chunks
Apple slices
Banana slices
Melon chunks or balls
And sprinkle with blueberries

Or fill melon shells with melon balls including other melons, if available.

Top with whipped cream sprinkled with nutmeg.

Pineapple Halves

Cut pineapple in half lengthwise (leaving on green top and cut in half with pineapple). Remove core, cutting it out lengthwise, and cut around inside walls of shell; then slit pineapple into wedges and remove to a bowl to be mixed with other fruits, such as:

Fresh or frozen blueberries
Strawberries
Cherries
Grapes
Apple chunks
Papaya chunks
Banana slices
Kiwi slices
Orange or mandarin segments

Kiwi Fruit

Garnish with mint leaves, whipped cream, or yogurt.

Grapefruit Halves

Cut grapefruit in half, place one round slice of peeled orange on top and one round slice of banana in center of orange slice. Top with 1 tablespoon yogurt flavored with ⅛ teaspoon cinamon and pinch of nutmeg.

Grapefruit shells may be filled with any and all fruits.

Garnishes

Yogurt seasoned with mace, nutmeg, cinnamon, or grated orange or lemon peel

Whipped cream with a little honey (optional) dabbed on top or put in a pastry tube and squeezed out decoratively around edge of shell or dish

Mint or other plant leaves and flowers

Cheese balls: Make balls out of cream cheese and roll in ground nuts, sesame seeds, or poppy seeds

Whole, chopped, or ground nuts or soybeans

Wheat germ

Fruit Gelatin

¼ cup cold water
1 tablespoon pure gelatin
½ cup boiling water
1 cup orange juice or ½ cup orange juice and
    ½ cup pineapple juice
1¼ cups fruit, cut up (fresh oranges, grapefruit, bananas, seedless grapes, pitted cherries, apples, etc. or canned pineapple chunks. Fresh pineapple will not jell.)

Soften gelatin in cold water and dissolve in boiling water. Cool.

Add fruit juice, and when it begins to set, stir in fruit.

Pour into shallow pan or 4 individual molds. If molds are used, a little fruit may be put in the bottom of each and the partially set gelatin carefully poured over the fruit.

Chill for 4 hours or until firm.

Serves 4

Fruit Gelatin

2 cups cold water
½ cup pure gelatin
3 cups boiling water
6 cups orange juice
3 cups pineapple juice
2 cups unsweetened, canned pineapple chunks
8 cups assorted fresh fruits, cut up (oranges, grapefruit, bananas, seedless grapes, pitted cherries, apples, etc.)

Soften gelatin in cold water and dissolve in boiling water. Cool.

Add fruit juice, and when it begins to set, stir in fruit.

Pour into shallow pans or individual molds which have been rinsed in cold water. If molds are used, a little fruit may be put in the bottom of each and the partially set gelatin carefully poured over the fruit.
Serves 50

Chunky Applesauce

8 apples
2 cups water
Mace, cinnamon, or nutmeg

Cut apples into quarters, peel, and core. Cut into large chunks.

Combine apples with water and cook 8 minutes until tender, not mushy.

Add a dash of spice and serve. If apples are too tart, a little honey may be added.
Serves 6

Grapefruit Ambrosia

1 grapefruit
Honey
Ground soybeans, almonds, or pecans

Cut grapefruit in half. Drizzle a little honey on each half and sprinkle with ground nuts.

Place under broiler and lightly brown.

Serves 2

Grapefruit and Strawberry Compote

3 large grapefruit
1½ cups strawberries
1 tablespoon orange juice
1 teaspoon lemon juice
1 tablespoon honey
6 whole unhulled strawberries

Peel and section the grapefruit and arrange the sections in compotes.

Wash the strawberries and remove hulls, then crush the strawberries and put them through a sieve.

Add orange juice, lemon juice, and honey. Mix well and spoon the purée over the grapefruit sections.

Garnish each with a whole unhulled strawberry, washed.

Frozen strawberries may be used if the fresh are unavailable.
Serves 6

Cakes

Cornell Enriched Birthday Layer Cake

2 cups unbleached flour, sift before measuring
3 tablespoons soy flour, sift before measuring
3 tablespoons noninstant nonfat dry milk
½ teaspoon sea salt
2½ teaspoons baking powder
2 tablespoons wheat germ
½ cup honey
1 cup butter, softened
4 eggs, separated
1½ teaspoons pure vanilla extract
1 cup milk

Preheat oven to 350°.

Sift together twice: flours, dry milk, salt, and baking powder. Stir in wheat germ.

Blend honey and softened butter, beat in egg yolks one at a time, and add vanilla.

Add flour mixture alternately with milk, stirring until smooth after each addition.

Beat egg whites until stiff but not dry and fold into batter.

Pour into 3 well-buttered 9″ layer pans and bake at 350° for 30 to 35 minutes or until an inserted toothpick comes out clean.

Cool on rack and frost with Carob Frosting (double recipe) (page 232).

Apples

Applesauce–Oatmeal Cake

1¼ cups unsweetened applesauce
¾ cup rolled oats
1 cup rye flour, sift before measuring
¼ cup soy flour, sift before measuring
2 tablespoons noninstant nonfat dry milk
1 tablespoon nutritional yeast
1½ tablespoons baking powder
1 teaspoon cinnamon
¼ cup honey
½ cup butter, softened
1 egg

Combine applesauce and oats in a saucepan and heat through. Set aside to cool.

Preheat oven to 350°.

Sift together flours, dry milk, yeast, baking powder, and cinnamon.

Stir honey into butter, beat in egg, and stir into dry mixture.

Stir in applesauce-oatmeal mixture and turn into buttered 9″ square pan. Bake at 350° for 50 minutes or until an inserted toothpick comes out clean.

Cool on rack.

Maple Sponge Cake

4 eggs
2 egg yolks
1 cup pure maple syrup
¼ cup milk
3 tablespoons butter
2 cups rye flour
2 tablespoons arrowroot
½ teaspoon sea salt
1 teaspoon baking powder
1 teaspoon pure vanilla extract

Preheat oven to 375°.

Place eggs, egg yolks, and maple syrup in top of double boiler. Place over hot water and beat with electric beater only until foamy; do not cook. Remove from heat.

Heat milk with butter and pour half of it into egg mixture; reserve other half.

Beat mixture in double boiler on low speed until thickened but not to the point of a custard consistency.

Sift the flour, returning particles in sifter to flour, and measure out 1 cup. Sift again with arrowroot, salt, and baking powder, returning any particles in sifter to bowl.

Pour egg mixture slowly into flour mixture while stirring. Add remaining milk-butter mixture and vanilla. Pour into two 9''x5'' loaf pans which have been prepared with pieces of wax paper cut to fit the bottoms. Butter the paper and sides of pans well.

Bake at 375° for 30 to 35 minutes or until an inserted toothpick comes out clean.

Cool on rack and serve with whipped cream and fruit or vanilla ice cream.

Strawberry Shortcake

1½ cups whole-wheat pastry flour
¼ cup oat flour
¼ cup cornstarch
2 tablespoons noninstant nonfat dry milk
½ teaspoon sea salt
1 teaspoon baking powder
¼ cup butter
2 eggs
⅔ cup milk
½ cup honey
1 quart strawberries, hulled and sliced, reserving 5
    whole berries for garnish
½ pint cream, whipped

Preheat oven to 450°.

Sift whole-wheat flour before measuring and return particles in sifter to the flour.

Sift together: flours, cornstarch, dry milk, salt, and baking powder. Cut in butter with 2 knives or pastry blender.

Beat eggs until light and stir in milk and honey.

Stir liquid ingredients into flour mixture and pour into buttered 9″ or 10″ layer pan.

Bake at 450° for 20 minutes or until an inserted toothpick comes out clean. Cool on rack.

Before serving, remove cake from pan and split cake in half. Cover lower half with half of the strawberry slices; place top layer of cake on and cover with remaining berries. Top with whipped cream and garnish with whole berries.

Serves 9

Note: The cake may be cut into individual servings before adding berries and cream. In this case, keep out 9 whole berries for garnish. Cut cake by thirds in both directions and then split each portion in half.

Chinese Sponge Cakes

3 eggs, separated
3 tablespoons honey
¾ cup rye flour, sifted
½ teaspoon baking powder

Preheat oven to 325°.

Beat egg yolks until light; add honey and continue beating. Add whites to yolks and beat for 3 minutes with electric beater.

Sift flour and baking powder together 3 times, returning any particles in sifter to bowl. Fold into egg mixture.

Spoon into buttered custard cups, half-full. Set in pan of boiling water about 1 inch deep. Cover with aluminum foil and bake at 325° for 35 minutes.

Serve with warm fruit sauce (see page 57), applesauce with cinnamon, or a little warmed pure maple syrup.
Serves 6

Carob Frosting

⅓ tablespoon butter
⅔ cup noninstant nonfat dry milk
⅓ cup sifted carob powder
3 tablespoons honey
¼ cup milk
1 teaspoon pure vanilla extract

Work butter into dry milk with fingertips. Add carob powder and beat in honey, milk, and vanilla.
Frosts 1 cake

Carob Butter Frosting

¼ cup butter, softened
3 tablespoons sifted carob powder
1 teaspoon pure vanilla extract

Blend butter, carob powder, and vanilla together with a wire whisk over cold water until spreading consistency.
Yield: ⅔ cup

Honey Meringue Frosting

1¼ cups honey
⅛ teaspoon salt
¼ teaspoon pure vanilla extract
2 egg whites

Cook honey with salt until it spins a thread when dripped from a spoon or until it forms a soft ball in cold water. This takes 30 to 40 minutes or more.

When the honey nears the threading stage, beat egg whites until stiff.

As soon as honey threads, pour in a thin stream over egg whites, beating constantly. Add vanilla and continue beating until right consistency for spreading. The frosting will get very thick and manageable.

Frosts a 2-layer cake

Caution: Honey Meringue Frosting is extremely sweet and should be used only sparingly and eaten infrequently.

The most wholesome frosting is whipped cream (which may be slightly sweetened with a little honey, although sweetening is usually unnecessary) topped with any of the following:

Garnish for Frosted Cakes

Fresh berries or sliced fresh fruit such as oranges or kiwi, arranged overlapping or with edges touching in a circle
Sliced bananas
Almond slivers, browned in butter
Whole pecan halves
Toasted sesame or sunflower seeds
Ground roasted soybeans
Ground almonds, pecans, or walnuts
Mace, cinnamon, or nutmeg
Carob powder, sifted
Toasted wheat germ

Pecan Nuts

Cookies

Rich Carob Brownies

    1 cup whole-wheat pastry flour
    ¾ cup sifted carob powder
    2 tablespoons rice polish
    ½ teaspoon sea salt
    1 cup chopped nuts
    4 eggs
    ½ cup unsulphured molasses
    ½ cup (¼ pound) butter, melted
    2 teaspoons pure vanilla extract

Preheat oven to 325°.

Sift flour before measuring and return any particles left in sifter to bowl.

Sift carob powder, forcing lumps through sieve, before measuring.

Sift together flour, carob powder, rice polish, and salt. Stir in nuts.

Beat eggs until light and add molasses, butter, and vanilla. Stir in dry ingredients, combining well, and pour into buttered 9″ square pan.

Bake at 325° for 30 to 35 minutes, depending upon how chewy you like your brownies. Cool and cut into fifths both directions. *Yield: 25*

Sesame Seeds

Granola Cookies

1 cup safflower oil or melted butter
1 egg
¼ cup honey
1 teaspoon pure vanilla extract
2 cups whole-wheat flour
¼ cup noninstant nonfat dry milk
½ teaspoon sea salt
2½ cups granola (see page 39)

Preheat oven to 325°.

Combine oil, egg, honey, and vanilla.

Add remaining ingredients and place by teaspoonful on buttered baking sheet. Press down to flatten.

Bake at 325° for 15 minutes. Cool on paper toweling to absorb excess oil or butter.
Yield: 48

Oat–Peanut Butter Cookies

4 eggs (5 small)
1 cup oat flour
1 teaspoon vanilla
1½ teaspoons sea salt
1 cup 100-percent peanut butter
1 cup sesame seeds
1 teaspoon baking powder
1 tablespoon oil or melted butter
Dash of cinnamon

Preheat oven to 375°.

Beat eggs slightly with whisk. Add remaining ingredients. Form balls, using 1 teaspoon of batter for each.

Press onto buttered baking sheet and bake at 375° for 10 to 12 minutes or until lightly browned.
Yield: 48

Quick Oatmeal Drop Cookies

2½ cups rolled oats
1¼ cups oat flour
¼ cup noninstant nonfat dry milk
½ teaspoon sea salt
1 cup safflower oil
½ cup honey
2 eggs
2 teaspoons pure vanilla extract
½ cup chopped nuts, or whole raisins.

Preheat oven to 350°.

Combine all ingredients and drop by teaspoon onto a buttered baking sheet.

Bake at 350° for 10 to 12 minutes.
Yield: 48

Oats

Banana Cookies

1 cup sesame seeds
1 cup whole-wheat flour
1 cup brown rice flour
1 teaspoon sea salt
1 teaspoon baking powder
½ teaspoon cinnamon
¾ cup butter
1 cup honey
1 egg
1 cup mashed banana
1 teaspoon pure vanilla extract

Preheat oven to 350°.

Put sesame seeds in a dry skillet and cook, stirring, until lightly browned. They will pop a little.

Sift flours and salt together and combine with baking powder and cinnamon.

Blend the honey and butter together until smooth. Beat in the egg and then beat in the mashed banana.

Add the dry mixture to honey mixture a third at a time, mixing well with each addition. Add sesame seeds and vanilla.

Drop by teaspoon onto a buttered cookie sheet and bake at 350° for 8 to 10 minutes.
Makes 25–35

Rice–Almond Cookies

⅔ cup safflower oil
¼ cup honey
2 eggs
1 teaspoon nutmeg
1½ cups ground almonds
½ teaspoon grated orange peel
2 tablespoons rice polish
3 cups brown rice flour (approximately)

Preheat oven to 350°.

Combine oil, honey, eggs, nutmeg, almonds, orange peel, and rice polish. Add flour gradually until right consistency to shape 2 long rolls 1½ inches thick. Refrigerate overnight or put in freezer for 2 to 3 hours.

Cut rolls into ¼-inch slices or roll out and cut various shapes with cookie cutter. Place on buttered baking sheet and bake at 350° for 10 to 12 minutes.
Yield: 48

Note: These cookies are flat and may be decorated if desired.

If a less grainy consistency is desired, use 2 cups whole-wheat pastry flour and 1 cup brown rice flour instead of all brown rice flour. Many people, however, prefer the interesting texture achieved with the use of brown rice flour alone.

Pies and Puddings

Unbaked Pie Shells

¾ cup whole-grain cracker crumbs
¼ cup wheat germ
¼ cup ground nuts
⅓ cup oil or melted butter
1 tablespoon honey

Combine all ingredients and press into pie pan.

¾ cup wheat germ
¾ cup whole-grain bread crumbs
½ cup melted butter

Combine all ingredients and press into pie pan.

Basic Pie Crust for Baked Pie Recipes

1 cup whole-wheat pastry flour
1 cup oat flour
1 teaspoon sea salt
½ cup butter
Ice water

Preheat oven to 400°.

Sift flours before measuring and combine with salt. Cut butter coarsely into flours with 2 knives or pastry blender.
With a fork, add enough ice water to make a dough.

Divide dough, leaving one half a little larger than the other.

Roll small half out on floured board, or between sheets of wax paper, making a round to fit the bottom of your pie pan.
Fill with desired filling and roll out other half on floured board, or between wax paper, making a slightly larger round to cover top of pie. Seal edges, flute, and bake.

Yield: 2 crusts

Note: Basic Pie Crust dough may be used for small individual pie shells by using an inverted muffin tin or custard cups. Cut the dough into 4½- 5½-inch rounds and fit them over the cups.

Prick the dough and bake at 325° for 25 to 30 minutes or until lightly browned.

Carob Pudding or Pie Filling

6 tablespoons sifted carob powder
¼ cup boiling water
1 package (1 tablespoon) pure, unflavored gelatin
2 tablespoons cornstarch
2 cups milk
4 tablespoons honey
3 egg yolks, slightly beaten
3 egg whites
2 tablespoons honey
½ cup whipping cream
1 teaspoon pure vanilla extract
½ cup chopped nuts

Put sifted carob powder in a bowl, add ¼ cup boiling water, and stir until smooth. Set aside.

Mix gelatin and cornstarch in a pan and add the milk and honey. Bring to a boil, stirring constantly. Stir in carob mixture and remove from heat.

Add a little of the hot mixture to the beaten egg yolks and stir into carob mixture. Return the pan to the heat and cook 1 minute. Pour into a large bowl and cool until slightly thickened.

Beat the egg whites until stiff. Gradually beat in 2 tablespoons of honey (it falls in a thin stream from the measuring spoon) and the vanilla. Whip the cream until it forms peaks.

Fold the egg whites into the carob mixture. Then fold in the whipping cream. Pour into a quart soufflé dish or dessert bowl. Sprinkle with chopped nuts and refrigerate until set.
Serves 6

Note: Or fill two unbaked pie shells (page 238), sprinkle with nuts, and refrigerate until set.
Serves 10–12.

Apple Pie

Basic Pie Crust for Baked Pies
4 cups peeled and sliced tart apples
¼ cup honey
½ teaspoon cinnamon
1½ tablespoons oat flour

Preheat oven to 400°.

Combine all ingredients, tossing well to cover apples.

Place bottom pie crust in pie pan and fill with apples.

Place top crust over apples, seal edges, and flute. Prick with a fork in several places to allow steam to escape.

Bake at 400° for 40 to 45 minutes or until lightly browned.

Steamed Fig or Date Pudding

1¾ cup whole-wheat pastry flour
¼ teaspoon sea salt
1½ teaspoons baking powder
1 teaspoon ginger powder
1 egg, beaten
¼ cup butter, softened
⅔ cup unsulphured molasses
⅔ cup milk
1 cup figs or dates, chopped fine

Sift flour to measure, returning any particles left in sifter to the bowl.

Then sift together flour, salt, baking powder, and ginger.

Beat egg until foamy and beat in butter, which will break up into little pieces. Stir in molasses and milk.

Add dry ingredients to the liquid ingredients and stir in fruit.

Pour into a well-oiled 1-quart mold with tight lid and steam for 3 hours. Be sure to check boiling water and add more when needed.

Serve with hard sauce.

Hard Sauce

⅓ cup butter
¾ cup honey
1 teaspoon pure vanilla extract

Beat honey into butter in a stream and beat in vanilla. Refirgerate until ready for use.
Serves 8

Note: This dessert is very sweet. Serve in small portions after a well-balanced meal.

Honey Custard

2 cups milk
2 tablespoons honey
3 eggs
¼ teaspoon sea salt
Nutmeg
Fresh fruit or berries.

Preheat oven to 325°.

Scald milk and stir the honey into it. Beat the eggs slightly and add the salt. Combine milk with the eggs and pour into 6 custard cups. Sprinkle with nutmeg.

Set the cups in a pan of hot water and bake at 350° for 40 to 45 minutes or until an inserted toothpick comes out clean.

Chill and serve with sliced fruit or berries.
Serves 6

German Dessert Pancakes

¼ cup butter
3 eggs
¾ cup milk
½ cup rye flour
¼ cup cornstarch
2-3 cups fresh fruit or Chunky Applesauce

Preheat oven to 425°.

Use 2- to 3-quart skillet or oval baking dish (measure size of pan by filling with quarts of water).

Place pan in oven with butter in it.

Put eggs, milk, flour, and cornstarch in blender and blend 1 minute.

Pour into hot dish on top of melted butter, and bake at 425° for 20 to 25 minutes. The batter will rise around the edges and puff a little in the center.

Remove from oven and fill with 2 to 3 cups hot fresh fruit or hot Chunky Applesauce (page 227). Sprinkle with nutmeg or cinnamon.

Serves 4

Note: To serve 6, use 3- to 4-quart dish or skillet and ⅓ cup butter, 4 eggs, 1 cup milk, ¾ cup rye flour, and ¼ cup cornstarch.

Quince

Icecream
Walnuts
Kumquats
Mango
Blueberries

Drinks, Snacks, and Refreshments

Carrots
Mung Beans & Sprouts
Tomato Fruit Juice
Apples
Grapes
Sesame Seeds
SESAME SEEDS

Nutritious drinks, snacks, and refreshments play an essential role in the health of each one of us and our families. This is true not only because they provide vital body-building properties, but because they take the place of non-nutritive and harmful drinks, snacks, and refreshments, which lead to much of the ill health in our country today.

Again we must consider only pure food—real food. We should avoid imitation dairy products and artificial colors, flavors, and sweeteners for the simple reason that our internal environment is neither imitation nor artificial; it is very real and is designed to handle and benefit by that which is very real. Eating real food, whenever we eat, is a part of God's exquisite formula for our health and growth.

Refreshment time gives us the supreme opportunity to present good nutrition to others and encourage one another to eat the foods God provided for our physical and mental health.

Drinks

There are many delicious and healthful hot drinks on the market. You will find a large variety of herb teas at natural food stores, many of which are good served iced as well. They also serve as a base for fruit punches. You will find interesting grain drinks to replace coffee. They are also good iced.

The quality of water is important. It is often overlooked because we are in the habit of drinking water that is full of chemicals; these chemicals affect both the nutritive value of the water and certainly the flavor. Tap water can ruin the flavor of a lovely nutritious drink; whereas, spring water and mineral waters bring us many valuable minerals in a pure form intended for our bodies. Furthermore, the quality of water becomes essential to all who are replacing soft drinks with healthful drinks because they will consume a great deal more water than in the past. The amount of chemicals put in water is based partially upon the estimate of the average consumption per person per day. When one sees the number of pop bottles being sold and returned in supermarkets, one gets a good idea of how many soft drinks are consumed a day by most families. Also, spring water has the added advantage of being cheaper. Colas cost four to five times as much as spring water. Think how much fresh lemonade and orangeade one can make at home quite reasonably!

The following combinations of drinks may be beaten together with a wire whisk or put in a blender. Try them and devise your own favorite nutritious drinks. Use them between meals for a snack and serve them for refreshments. The milk, yogurt, fruit, and vegetable drinks which are fortified with wheat germ, rice polish, soy powder, nonfat dry milk, nutritional yeast, eggs, protein powder, seeds, and nuts are especially nourishing and suitable for lunch pails and brown bags. They may be enjoyed with lunch or as mid-morning or mid-afternoon snacks.

Milk Drinks

Milk drinks may be made of cow's milk, goat's milk, or soy milk. Soy milk may be made by beating 6 tablespoons of soy milk powder into 2 cups water. Refrigerate soy milk. Milk drinks can also be made with buttermilk and yogurt.

Use blender or electric beater.

Variety may be given to milk drinks with the addition of:

> Carob powder
> Fruit
> Ice cream—made of wholesome ingredients
> Sherbet—made of wholesome ingredients

Milk drinks may be nutritionally fortified with:

> Wheat germ
> Rice polish
> Nutritional yeast
> Noninstant nonfat dry milk
> Seeds: sesame, sunflower, pumpkin
> Nuts, ground
> Soy powder
> Soybeans, ground
> Lecithin

Safflower oil
Protein powder
Desiccated liver powder
Eggs
Bran flakes
Flaxseed
Nut butters and tahini (sesame butter)
Sprouts

Milk drinks may be flavored with:

Pure vanilla extract
Pure almond extract
Pure fruit concentrates

Milk shakes may be sweetened with:

Honey
Maple syrup
Unsulphured molasses
Chopped dates
Chopped figs
Raisins
Banana flakes and other dried fruit flakes

Specific examples are as follows:

★ Blend ¼ cup sesame or sunflower seeds, 1 tablespoon carob powder, and 6 pitted dates with 2 cups milk. *Serves 2–3*

★ Blend 1 teaspoon wheat germ and 2 teaspoons ground peanuts with 2 cups milk; add 1 teaspoon honey and blend again. *Serves 2–3*

★ Blend 1 cut-up ripe banana, ¼ cup noninstant nonfat dry milk, ½ teaspoon cinnamon, and 2 teaspoons peanut butter with 2 cups of milk. *Serves 3–4*

★ Blend ¼ cup soy flour, 1 tablespoon nutritional yeast, 1 tablespoon lecithin powder, 1 tablespoon safflower oil, 2 eggs, and ½ teaspoon pure vanilla extract with 2 cups milk. *Serves 4–6*

★ Blend 1 cup fresh berries, 1 tablespoon honey, pinch of sea salt, and 2 cups milk. *Serves 4–6*

★ Blend 4 eggs, ¼ cup noninstant nonfat dry milk, 2 tablespoons wheat germ, 1 cup orange juice, and 2 cups milk. *Serves 4–6*

★ Blend 3 tablespoons carob powder, 2 tablespoons noninstant nonfat dry milk, 1 tablespoon honey, 2 cups milk, and 1 teaspoon pure vanilla extract. *Serves 2*

★ Blend 2 ripe bananas, 2 tablespoons rice polish, 6 chopped dates, 2 tablespoons protein powder, and 2 cups milk. *Serves 2–3*

★ Blend 2 cups orange juice, 1 tablespoon honey, and 2 cups buttermilk. Chill. *Serves 4*

★ Blend 2 cups blueberries, 2 cups buttermilk, 2 teaspoons lecithin granules, 1 teaspoon honey, and ½ teaspoon nutmeg. *Serves 2–3*

★ Blend ½ cup yogurt, 1 cup soy powder, ½ cup wheat germ, 1 teaspoon sesame seeds, 1 teaspoon pure vanilla extract, and 4 cups milk. *Serves 4–5*

★ Blend 1 cup tomato juice, 2 cups yogurt, 2 teaspoons minced onion, 1 crushed garlic clove, ½ teaspoon sea salt, ¼ teaspoon kelp powder, and ¼ teaspoon caraway seeds (optional). *Serves 3–4*

★ Blend 4 eggs, ½ cup yogurt, ½ cup wheat germ, 2 tablespoons safflower oil, 1 cup noninstant nonfat dry milk, ¾ cups soy milk powder, 4 cups water, and 2 teaspoons pure vanilla extract. *Serves 4–6*

Figs

Nut Milks

★ 1 cup ground peanuts, cashews, or almonds, 4 cups water, and 2 tablespoons honey. Also good made with apple juice. *Serves 4–6*

Fruit Drinks

Fruit drinks may be made of any fruit juice.
Use blender or electric beater.

Orange	Pear
Grapefruit	Apple
Tangelo	Lemon
Lime	Pineapple
Grape, pure white or purple	Boysenberry
Papaya	Cherry
Apricot	

Combined or used separately with the addition of diced fresh or unsweetened frozen fruit, such as:

Strawberries	Peaches
Raspberries	Apricots
Blueberries	Papayas
Blackberries	Avocados
Bananas	Grapes
Cranberries	Pomegranates
Apples	Pineapple
Pears	

They may be sweetened, if needed, with a small amount of:

Honey
Unsulphured molasses
Barley malt
Chopped dates
Chopped figs
Raisins
Banana flakes and other dried fruit flakes

Fruit drinks may be nutritionally fortified further with the addition of the following:

Seeds: sesame, sunflower, pumpkin
Sprouts of all kinds
Ground nuts
Nut butters and tahini (sesame paste)

Wheat germ
Rice polish
Nutritional yeast
Lecithin granules
Noninstant nonfat dry milk
Bran flakes
Flaxseed
Soybeans, roasted and ground
Soy milk powder
Eggs
Yogurt
Oils, cold pressed or unrefined
Wholesome ice cream or sherbet

Interesting seasonings for fruit drinks are as follows:

Mace
Nutmeg
Cinnamon
Grated lemon peel
Grated orange peel
Mint, fresh or dried
Cardamon
Anise

Specific examples are as follows. *Use blender or electric beater.*

★ Blend 3 ripe avocados with 3⅓ cups unsweetened grapefruit juice and 2 tablespoons honey. Chill and pour over ice. *Serves 6–8*

★ Blend 2 avocados with 2 cups yogurt, 1 tablespoon lemon juice, and 2 tablespoons nonfat dry milk. Chill. *Serves 4*

★ Blend 3 avocados with 3¾ cups orange juice and 1 tablespoon toasted sesame seeds. *Serves 6*

★ Blend 4 cups natural, unsweetened apple juice, 1 cup orange juice, 1 cup pineapple juice, ¼ cup lemon juice, and ¼ cup fresh or unsweetened frozen strawberries. *Serves 6*

★ Blend 2 cups orange juice, 4 chopped dates, and 1 egg. *Serves 2*

★ 1 quart orange juice, 1 quart grapefruit juice, 1 quart pineapple juice, and 1 quart unsweetened cranberry juice poured over ice. Ice cream, sherbet, or fresh fruit may be added. *Serves 15–20*

★ Use the above recipe along with 2 quarts lemonade (sweetened with barley malt) and 2 quarts mineral water. A little more honey may be added, if desired. The orange juice and grapefruit juice may be frozen juice diluted with 1 can to 3 cans water. *Serves 50*

★ Eight tablespoons herb tea steeped in 2 gallons boiling water for 6 to 10 minutes; stir in ½ cup honey and stir until dissolved. Cool and add the juice of 8 lemons and 1 gallon water. Stir and pour over ice. Garnish with fresh mint or lemon slices. *Serves 50*

★ Blend 1 cup orange juice, 1 tablespoon wheat germ, 1 tablespoon noninstant nonfat dry milk, 1 tablespoon lecithin granules, 1 teaspoon flaxseed, 1 teaspoon bran flakes, 1 tablespoon safflower oil, and 1 egg. (Any fruit juice may be used.) *Serves 1*

★ Blend 1 cup pineapple juice, 2 cut-up peaches, 1 tablespoon noninstant nonfat dry milk, and 1 teaspoon ground almonds (optional). *Serves 1*

★ Blend 1 cut-up ripe papaya, ½ cup orange juice, and ½ cup yogurt. *Serves 1*

★ Blend ½ cup fresh or frozen blueberries, 1 cup yogurt, 1 teaspoon noninstant nonfat dry milk, and 1 teaspoon honey. *Serves 1*

★ Blend 1 cup orange juice, ½ cup fresh or frozen strawberries, 1 tablespoon lemon juice, and 1 teaspoon honey. *Serves 1*

★ Blend 1 cup unsweetened pineapple juice, ½ cup melon chunks, and ½ teaspoon dried or fresh mint leaves. *Serves 1*

Oranges

★ Blend ¼ cup peanuts or sesame seeds and 1 cup water; then add 1 cut up banana, and the juice of 1 orange and blend a minute more. *Serves 1*

★ Blend ½ cup unsweetened cranberry juice, ½ cup natural, unsweetened apple juice, 1 teaspoon lime or lemon juice, 1 teaspoon noninstant nonfat dry milk, 1 teaspoon sunflower seeds, and 1 egg. *Serves 1*

★ Blend the juice of ½ lime with the juice of either ½ lemon, tangerine, tangelo, or orange and 1 cup water. *Serves 1*

★ Blend 1 cup unsweetened pineapple juice and 2 heaping tablespoons soy powder. *Serves 1*

★ Blend 2 cups pineapple juice, 1½ tablespoons lemon juice, 2 egg yolks, 1 tablespoon honey, pinch sea salt, and ¼ cup crushed ice. *Serves 3–4*

Lemonade–Pineapple Punch for 100

Boil together 4 cups water and 8 cups honey for 10 minutes. Cool the syrup and add 8 cups lemon juice, 2 no. 2½ cans unsweetened crushed pineapple, 8 sliced oranges, and 4 gallons water. Serve over ice. Garnish with mint or lemon slices.

Vegetable Drinks

May be made by blending vegetable juices or vegetable and fruit juices and/or vegetables themselves. They may be served at the beginning of a meal or instead of salad at lunch and are excellent to send along in lunch pails and brown bags.

It is simple and enjoyable to devise your own vegetable drinks. The following suggestions of ingredients will give you a start. Let your taste be your guide. *Use blender or electric beater.*

Some of the vegetables and other juices or stocks that lend themselves especially well to vegetable drinks are:

Tomato juice
Celery juice
Sauerkraut juice
Carrot juice
Water in which vegetables have been cooked
Water in which sprouting seeds have been soaked
Clam juice
Chicken or beef stock
Orange juice
Pineapple juice
Grapefruit juice
Papaya juice
Apple juice, natural and unfiltered

Vegetable juices may be obtained from natural food stores or prepared at home in a special juice extractor. Some of the vegetables which may be added to vegetable juice drinks are:

Lettuce	Minced onion or shallots
Watercress	Chopped parsley
Shaved carrot	Diced cucumber
Diced celery	Tomato
Sprouts	Minced green pepper
Spinach	Shredded cabbage
Peas	Corn kernels
Grated beet	

Some of the seasonings which may be added to vegetable drinks are:

Herbs: basil, marjoram, sage, thyme, etc.
Kelp
Vegetable salt
Sea salt
Minced onion or shallots
Garlic clove, crushed
Curry powder
Worcestershire sauce

Sage tea
Lemon or lime juice

Vegetable drinks may be nutritionally fortified further with the addition of the following:

Seeds: sesame, sunflower, pumpkin
Nuts, ground
Noninstant nonfat dry milk
Nutritional yeast
Lecithin
Desiccated liver powder
Wheat germ
Rice polish
Bran flakes
Flaxseed
Yogurt
Soybeans, roasted and ground
Soy milk powder
Protein powder
Nut butters or tahini (sesame seed paste)

Specific examples are as follows. *Use blender or electric beater.*

★ Blend 1 cup tomato juice, ½ cup sauerkraut juice, ¼ teaspoon vegetable salt, 1 teaspoon chopped parsley, and 1 teaspoon nutritional yeast. *Serves 1*

★ Blend 1 cup tomato juice, ½ avocado cut up, 1 slice onion, minced, and ⅛ teaspoon sea salt. *Serves 1*

★ 1 cup tomato juice, ¼ cup carrot juice, ¼ cup celery juice, 1 teaspoon chopped parsley, and ⅛ teaspoon vegetable salt. *Serves 1*

★ 1 cup tomato juice, 1 slice onion minced, 2 tablespoons raw or cooked peas or diced beans, and a pinch of basil and marjoram. *Serves 1*

★ 4 ripe tomatoes peeled, 1 teaspoon minced onion, ⅛ teaspoon garlic powder, and ½ teaspoon sea salt. *Serves 2*

★ 4 cups tomato juice, 1 lettuce leaf, 1 tablespoon chopped green pepper, 1 stalk celery with leaves chopped, and ½ teaspoon vegetable salt. *Serves 4*

★ 1 cup carrot juice, ¼ cup unsweetened pineapple juice, and ¼ cup wheat germ. *Serves 1*

★ 2 cups carrot juice, few sprigs watercress cut up, 1 tablespoon lemon juice, ½ cucumber chopped, and ¼ teaspoon sea salt. *Serves 2*

★ 1 cup carrot or celery juice, 1 raw beet, grated, ¼ teaspoon thyme, and ⅛ teaspoon sea salt. *Serves 1*

Snacks

The usual snacks today are appropriately known as "junk foods," even by those who are neither knowledgeable nor deeply concerned with good nutrition. And junk foods abound at every turn: snack bars, vending machines, and, most unfortunately, pantry shelves in homes. These foods are high in sugar, high in fat, high in artificial colorings and flavorings, and are most often made of depleted and altered foods. A concerted effort must be made to see that nutritious snacks are available. Have them around the house, send them to school and office, and take them on trips.

Some suggestions are as follows:

> Fresh fruit
> Fruit juices
> Raw vegetables, such as: celery, carrot, green pepper, zucchini, and turnip strips
> Vegetable juices
> Whole-grain breads and crackers
> Cheese and rice crackers
> Peanut butter and other nut butters
> Jams and jellies made of pure fruit and honey
> Cheeses of all kinds, including kefir cheese
> Popcorn
> Seeds: Sesame, sunflower, and pumpkin
> Roasted soybeans
> Nuts of all kinds
> Nutritious cookies
> Milk
> Milk drinks

Carob drink, hot or cold
Wholesome ice creams and sherbets
Dried fruit
Plain yogurt with fresh fruit
Mixtures of puffed whole wheat, puffed brown rice, puffed millet, nuts, and raisins
Mixtures of nuts, seeds, and dried fruit

An example of a nut-seed-dried fruit mixture is as follows:

1 cup pumpkin seeds
1 cup chopped unblanched almonds
1 cup soybeans
1 cup sunflower seeds
1 cup coarsely chopped pecans
1 cup coarsely chopped walnuts
2 teaspoons sea salt
1 cup banana flakes or other dried fruit flakes or raisins

Toss all ingredients together and serve, or toast for 10 to 12 minutes in a 400° oven and serve.

Note: Any nuts may be used: cashews, hazel nuts, pine nuts, peanuts, macadamia nuts, etc.

Refreshments

The following suggestions for refreshments may cover all occasions: "coffees," teas, and receptions.

Beverages
Sandwiches
Cakes and cookies
Breads, rolls, and biscuits

Following are recipes for canapes, hors d'oeuvres, and confections, as well as a recipe for fifty tea sandwiches.

Charlton Chicken Sandwiches

3 eggs
1 quart half-and-half cream
3 tablespoons butter
4 tablespoons brown rice flour
1 chicken, cooked and ground
Sea salt to taste

Beat the eggs and add the quart of cream.

Melt the butter, add the flour, and simmer 3 minutes. Stir in the egg-and-cream mixture.

Simmer until the consistency of cream sauce.

Add the ground chicken, salt to taste, and chill.

Cut the crusts off 50 thin slices of whole-grain bread.

Spread half of them with butter, then with the chicken spread, and top with remaining slices.

Cut into halves.

Yield: 50 tea sandwiches
Note: These freeze well because they do not contain any mayonnaise.

Pizzas

Whole-wheat bread dough (page 138)
8 to 10 slices Fontina or Mozzarella cheese
Tomato sauce (page 75) or Italian tomato paste
½ cup chopped green pepper
4 tablespoons sliced green onions, sautéed in butter
12 anchovies or slices of additive-free sausage
1 cup sliced, fresh mushrooms
½ cup pitted black olives
2 tablespoons unrefined olive oil
Italian herb seasoning or oregano
Grated Parmesan or Romano cheese

For each pizza use one-fourth whole-wheat bread dough recipe and the following filling.

Roll dough thinly to fit a 13″ to 14″ pizza pan or two 9″x12″ baking pans, pinching up a collar around the pans to hold the filling.

Spread slices of Fontina or Mozzarella cheese over dough before the sauce is added; this keeps the dough from getting soggy.

Preheat oven to 450°.

Spread tomato sauce or tomato paste over cheese and distribute over it any of the following: green pepper, onion, anchovies or sausage, mushrooms, and olives.

Sprinkle the entire surface with oil, herbs, and grated cheese.

Bake at 450° for 15 to 20 minutes.

Green Peppers

Canapes and Hors d'Oeuvres

French Stuffed Mushrooms

48 large mushrooms
½ cup flaked, cooked white fish, tuna, or minced chicken
1 garlic clove, minced
1 tablespoon chopped parsley
1 egg
Wheat germ
Butter

Preheat oven to 350°.

Remove mushroom stems, cut off bottom of stems, and clean caps and stems by wiping with a damp cloth.

Combine ½ cup minced stems with the fish or chicken, garlic, parsley, and egg.

Fill the mushroom caps with this mixture, sprinkle with wheat germ, and dot with butter.

Place on buttered baking pan and bake at 350° for 15 minutes.
Yield: 48

English Canapes

Whole Grains

2 cans skinless and boneless sardines
¼ cup butter, softened
2 teaspoons dry mustard
¼ teaspoon Worcestershire sauce
Wheat germ
5 slices whole-grain bread

Drain oil from cans and lift out sardines. Split them in half lengthwise.

Combine butter, mustard, and Worcestershire sauce and spread sardines with this mixture. Dip them in wheat germ.

Remove crusts from bread slices, toast them, and cut each into 4 strips. Place sardine half on each and broil for 3 to 5 minutes or until lightly browned.
Yield: 20

Syrian Eggplant

1 eggplant
Butter
¼ cup unrefined olive oil
¼ cup lemon juice
3 tablespoons chopped parsley
1 garlic clove, minced
1 small chopped green pepper
½ cup yogurt
10 to 15 slices dark bread

Peel eggplant, slice thin, sáute in butter on both sides, and cool.

Combine oil, lemon juice, parsley, garlic, green pepper, and yogurt. Marinate the eggplant slices in this mixture and chill.

Serve on thinly sliced dark bread.
Yield: 10–15

Indian Rice Balls

2 cups cooked brown rice
1 cup grated Cheddar cheese
Prepared mustard
Safflower oil

Mix rice and cheese together well and form into balls by the tablespoonful.

Spread prepared mustard on balls and fry in deep oil long enough to brown lightly.
Yield: 30–35

Chinese Shrimp

Shrimp
Tamari soy sauce

Dip shelled, cleaned shrimp in tamari and broil.

Serve on toothpicks.

Russian Chicken Liver Cups

½ pound butter
2 cups rye flour
1 tablespoon sour cream
12 chicken livers
Sour cream
Paprika

Preheat oven to 375°.

Cut butter into flour with two knives or pastry blender and add 1 tablespoon sour cream. Form into a ball, wrap in wax paper, and chill until firm.

Roll pastry out on a floured board and cut into 1½-inch circles. Pinch sides to form a cup and fill with chopped chicken livers moistened with a little sour cream.

Sprinkle with paprika and bake at 375° for 20 minutes.
Yield: 25–30

Swedish Shrimp

50 large, cooked shrimp
2 cups cider vinegar
2 bay leaves
1 tablespoon tarragon
8 peppercorns
2 teaspoons dill seed

Combine vinegar, bay leaves, tarragon, peppercorns, and dill seed. Marinate shrimp in this mixture.

To serve, drain shrimp, reserving marinade. Hang shrimp on the edge of a bowl filled with the shrimp maridade, to be used as a dip.
Yield: 50

Chicken, Tuna, or Crabmeat Puffs

1 cup boiling water
¼ pound butter
¾ cup rye flour
1 teaspoon sea salt
2 tablespoons arrowroot
4 eggs (5 small)
2 cups cooked minced chicken or flaked fish
1 tablespoon minced onion or shallots, optional
Mayonnaise

Preheat oven to 450°.

Melt butter in boiling water.

Combine flour, salt, and arrowroot and pour all at once into water with butter. Stir briskly until mixture leaves sides of pan.

Remove from heat and beat in eggs one at a time until each is completely blended.

Drop by teaspoonfuls on buttered baking sheet and bake at 450° for 10 minutes. Lower heat to 325° and bake 15 minutes longer.

Turn off oven, slit each puff on the side to let out steam, and return to oven to dry out 5 minutes.

Cool puffs and fill with minced chicken or flaked fish moistened with a little mayonnaise. One tablespoon minced onion may be added. Allow 1 tablespoon for each puff or more if desired.
Yield: 30

Cheese Cups

2 piecrusts (page 238) or 50 slices dark bread
50 slices Muenster cheese, each 1-inch square
Sour cream
50 pecan halves

Roll out piecrusts and cut into 50 1½-inch circles. Pinch edges to form cups and bake until lightly browned.

Place slice of cheese on each and top with a dab of sour cream and a pecan half. Serve at once.
Yield: 50

Cheese Balls

3 ounces cream cheese
3 ounces Roquefort or blue cheese, crumbled
1 tablespoon chopped chives
1 tablespoon chopped parsley
Ground nuts

Soften and combine cheeses. Chill and form into balls. Roll in nuts.
Yield: 15

Cheese Roll

3 ounces cream cheese
3 ounces Cheddar cheese, grated
3 ounces Roquefort or blue cheese, crumbled
Chopped nuts

Blend the cheeses together with a fork and form into a log.

Spread ground nuts on a piece of wax paper. Roll log over the nuts, wrap the paper around, and chill until firm.

To serve, slice in desired thickness.

Stuffed Eggs

Simmer as many eggs as desired for 12 minutes. Drain water and shake the pan until the shells are well cracked. Pour ice cold water over eggs immediately, and the shells will slip off easily.

Cut eggs in half lengthwise and scoop out yolks into a bowl. Combine with enough mayonnaise to moisten well and add any of the following seasonings:

> Sea salt
> Pepper
> Paprika
> Curry powder
> Chili powder
> Garlic powder
> Minced onion
> Onion powder
> Herbs (marjoram, basil, thyme, etc.)
> Seeds (sesame, sunflower, poppy, celery)
> Kelp granules or powder
> Mustard powder

Fill egg whites, heaping generously, and sprinkle with chopped parsley or paprika.

Stuffed Celery

Stuff celery stalks with any of the following mixtures:

Blend 3 ounces cream cheese with 1 tablespoon Roquefort or blue cheese, 1 tablespoon butter, and 1 teaspoon dill seed.

Blend 3 ounces cream cheese with 2 tablespoons sprouts and 1 teaspoon celery seed.

Blend 3 ounces cream cheese with 1 teaspoon minced onion, 1 tablespoon minced green pepper, and ½ teaspoon kelp powder.

Blend 3 ounces cream cheese with 2 tablespoons crushed unsweetened pineapple.

The above combinations may be spooned into the cavities of celery stalks or they may be forced through a pastry tube into the cavities.

Dips

★ Blend together 3 ripe avocados, 2 tomatoes peeled and chopped, 1 onion minced, ½ teaspoon chili powder, ½ teaspoon kelp powder, 1 tablespoon lemon juice, and ¼ cup yogurt.

★ Blend together 1 cup tofu (bean curd), 1 tablespoon minced onion, and 1 tablespoon tamari soy sauce.

★ Blend together 2 cups cooked garbanzo beans (chick peas), 3 tablespoons tahini (sesame paste), 3 cloves garlic crushed, 3 tablespoons lemon juice, and 2 teaspoons unrefined olive oil.

★ Blend together 1 cup yogurt, 2 tablespoons chopped chives, ¼ cup sunflower seeds, ½ cup chopped ripe olives, and ½ teaspoon sea salt.

★ Blend 1½ cups sour cream, 1 cup yogurt, 1 cup raw, chopped spinach, ¼ cup chopped parsley, ½ cup chopped chives, and 1 teaspoon sea salt.

★ Blend together 1 pint cottage cheese, ¼ cup chopped chives, and ½ teaspoon sea salt or to taste.

★ Blend 1 cup cottage cheese, 1 cup yogurt, 1 tablespoon minced onion, 2 tablespoons minced parsley, and ½ teaspoon sea salt.

Serve with whole-grain crackers or pieces of raw vegetables, such as:

> Carrot sticks
> Celery sticks
> Cauliflower buds
> Broccoli stem strips
> Turnip strips
> Jicama strips

Fresh Fruit

Platters of whole strawberries, fresh pineapple cubes, and melon cubes or balls dipped in lemon juice. Fruit may be speared with canape toothpicks.

Confections

Confections are easily made at home according to one's own taste. They are very sweet, however, so should be eaten sparingly and only occasionally.

Into a food chopper put such fruits as raisins, pitted dates or prunes, figs, and dried apricots, currants, peaches, and apples. Dried prunes, apricots, and peaches should be soaked for 5 minutes in boiling water before chopping. These fruits may be combined as desired and formed into rolls, then rolled in ground nuts or coconut, and cut into 1-inch slices.

Stuffed Prunes

Steam prunes for 5 minutes over boiling water, then cut in half and pit. They may be stuffed with chopped nuts mixed with a little honey, or with cream cheese mixed with chopped nuts or toasted sesame seeds.

Stuffed Dates

Split dates, pit, and stuff with peanut butter, plain or mixed with an equal amount of noninstant nonfat dry milk and a little honey. Dates may also be stuffed with cream cheese and chopped nuts.

Wheat Germ Confection

Combine 2 cups toasted wheat germ, ¾ cup noninstant nonfat dry milk, 1 cup peanut butter, and enough honey to make mixture hold together. Press into a buttered loaf pan, chill, and cut into desired pieces with a wet knife.

Carob Confection

Combine ⅓ cup sifted carob powder, ⅓ cup noninstant nonfat dry milk, ⅓ cup soy milk powder, ¼ cup butter, 2 tablespoons chopped peanuts, ¼ cup honey, and ½ teaspoon pure vanilla extract. Shape into small balls and roll in coconut, or omit peanuts and roll in ground nuts.

Date–Granola Balls

Put ¼ cup butter, ¼ cup honey, and ½ cup finely chopped dates in a saucepan and blend together over low heat. Stir in 1 cup granola and 2 tablespoons noninstant nonfat dry milk. Cool mixture and form little balls by the teaspoonful. Roll in ground nuts. Store in refrigerator.

(Our family considers these the best confection ever!)

Source Books and Recommended Reading

Cheraskin, E., and Ringsdorf, W. J. Jr. *Psycho-Dietetics: Food As the Key to Emotional Health*. New York: Stein and Day, 1974.

Cheraskin, et al. *Diet and Disease*. Emmaus, Pa.: Rodale Press, 1968.

Hall, Ross H. *Food for Nought: The Decline of Nutrition*. Rev. ed. New York: Harper and Row, 1974.

Hunter, Beatrice T. *Consumer Beware*. New York: Simon and Schuster, Inc., 1971.

———. *The Mirage of Safety*. New York: Charles Scribner's Sons, 1975.

Ogden, Samuel R. *Step by Step Guide to Organic Gardening*. Emmaus, Pa.: Rodale Press, Inc., 1971.

Renwick, Ethel H. *Let's Try Real Food*. Grand Rapids, Mich.: Zondervan Publishing House, 1976.

Verrett, Jacqueline, and Carper, Jean. *Eating May Be Hazardous to Your Health*. New York: Simon and Schuster, Inc., 1974.

Williams, Roger J. *Nutrition Against Disease*. New York: Pitman Publishing Corp., 1971.

———. *The Wonderful World Within You: Your Inner Nutritional Environment*. New York: Bantam Books, 1977.

Yudkin, John. *Sweet and Dangerous*. New York: Bantam Books, Inc., 1973.

Let's Live Magazine, 444 North Larchmont Boulevard, Los Angeles, Calif. 90004.

Organic Gardening and Farming Magazine, Rodale Press, Emmaus, Pa. 18049.

Prevention Magazine, Rodale Press, Emmaus, Pa. 18049.

The Organic Directory, Rodale Press, Emmaus, Pa. 18049. A national organic buying guide listing food stores, organic growers and distributors, and giving other information on choosing organic meats, eggs, vegetables, cereals, and grains.

A